BEYONCÉ

A Biography of a Legendary Singer

Michael A. Schuman

Enslow Publishers, Inc.
40 Industrial Road
Box 398
Berkeley Heights, NJ 07922
USA

http://www.enslow.com

Library of Congress Cataloging-in-Publication Data

Schuman, Michael.
    Beyoncé : a biography of a legendary singer / Michael A. Schuman.
        pages cm. — (African-American icons)
    Includes bibliographical references and index.
    Summary: "Discusses the life of legendary singer Beyoncé Knowles, including her childhood and family life, her rise to superstardom from a member of the group Destiny's Child to her remarkable solo career, and her success in movies and business" —Provided by publisher.
    ISBN 978-0-7660-4230-8
    1. Beyoncé, 1981—Juvenile literature. 2. Rhythm and blues musicians—United States—Biography—Juvenile literature. 3. Singers—United States—Biography—Juvenile literature. I. Title.
    ML3930.K66S38 2014
    782.42164092—dc23
    [B]
                                    2013010854
Future editions:
Paperback ISBN: 978-1-4644-0403-0
EPUB ISBN: 978-1-4645-1221-6
Single-User PDF ISBN: 978-1-4646-1221-3
Multi-User PDF ISBN: 978-0-7660-5853-8

Printed in the United States of America
112013 Lake Book Manufacturing, Inc., Melrose Park, IL
10 9 8 7 6 5 4 3 2 1

To Our Readers:
We have done our best to make sure all Internet addresses in this book were active and appropriate when we went to press. However, the author and the publisher have no control over and assume no liability for the material available on those Internet sites or on other Web sites they may link to. Any comments or suggestions can be sent by e-mail to comments@enslow.com or to the address on the back cover.

♻ Enslow Publishers, Inc., is committed to printing our books on recycled paper. The paper in every book contains 10% to 30% post-consumer waste (PCW). The cover board on the outside of each book contains 100% PCW. Our goal is to do our part to help young people and the environment too!

Cover Illustration: AP Images / Dan Steinberg

CONTENTS

Chapter 1

IT BEGAN WITH A DREAM

Even as a child in elementary school, Beyoncé Knowles dreamed of being a world-famous singer. She wanted so much to be able to belt out a song like Whitney Houston or command a stage like Michael Jackson. She was determined not to let anything stand in her way. In fact, she had her first taste of entertaining an audience when, as a child, she entered a talent show in her hometown of Houston, Texas. At an age when children are losing their baby teeth, Beyoncé was already thinking like a grown-up.

And she has succeeded beyond anyone's imagination. By 2011, she had recorded too many best-selling albums and single songs to mention in one breath. She had also acted in movies and is well known for donating her money and time to help needy people. She had received many Grammy and MTV awards for solo performances, albums, or songs. But in May 2011, she was about to receive what many would consider her greatest honor.

Billboard magazine is the most respected publication for those who work in the music business. *Billboard* awards musicians and singers annually for their accomplishments the previous year. Beyoncé was about to receive an award that *Billboard* had created just a year earlier. It did not honor a performer for a single song or album. It is the Millennium Award, given only to those whose entire careers are amazing. From 2003 through 2011, she had sold as a solo artist roughly 11 million albums and 25 million singles.[1] And she had done this all before her thirtieth birthday.

More than fifteen thousand people were in attendance at the MGM Grand Garden Arena in Las Vegas, Nevada. They watched as several awards were given that night. There were live performances from some of the hottest names in music, including Rihanna, the Black Eyed Peas, Keith Urban, Cee Lo

Green, and Nicki Minaj. And, of course, Beyoncé, who awed the audience with a rousing rendition of her newest song, "Run the World (Girls)." Most touching, however, were the tributes she received as she accepted the Millennium Award. Since not all the people paying tribute to Beyoncé could be there in person, many were videotaped earlier, and their comments were played back to Beyoncé and the audience in the sold-out arena.

Music superstars, including Lady Gaga and Bono, offered admiring words. Barbra Streisand, one of the world's most famous and respected singers, and more than twice Beyoncé's age, said, "Great performers have a sound and style that is all their own, and that's why so many people love Beyoncé. And so do I." Stevie Wonder praised her by saying, "Beyoncé has made history and she is not even 30 yet." He also admired her dignity by acknowledging, "She's able to go to many places but still keep that class. I like that." Rhythm-and-blues kingpin Kenneth "Babyface" Edmonds remarked, "She inspired me to want to be more of an artist."

However, the biggest celebrity to offer praise on videotape was the First Lady of the United States. Michelle Obama took time from her hectic schedule to tell the audience, "I'm very proud of her, very proud of the woman she is and the role model she provides to so many women. And I truly congratulate her on her success."

After receiving the award, Beyoncé told the crowd, "I would like to start off by thanking my foundation, which is my family. Mom, you have taught me everything I know by example. I'd like to thank my father for teaching me so much about the music industry and teaching me about drive, and teaching me about work ethic."

She also thanked her husband, recording artist Jay-Z. Beyoncé referred to him as "my best friend."

After taking in the honor and all the praise, Beyoncé gushed to the audience, "I thank all the legends who said all those beautiful things to me. I grew up loving and admiring the people who were on that tape. This is a moment I have to soak in because it is one of the best memories of my life."[2]

It was a long journey from Beyoncé's first talent show appearance in Houston to the glamorous MGM Grand Garden Arena in Las Vegas. But she made it, as she had always dreamed she would.

Chapter 2

"THAT CAN'T BE OUR BEYONCÉ"

Beyoncé Giselle Knowles was born in Houston, Texas, on September 4, 1981. Her father, Mathew, was a salesman for Xerox, a huge company that makes business supplies and computer components. Her mother, Tina, owned a hair salon.

Mathew is African American and Tina is mixed race. She is part Creole, a descendent of the colonial French settlers in Louisiana. She is also part African American, American Indian, and Jewish. Beyoncé's unusual first name is a variation of her mother's maiden name. Before she married, Tina's name was

Tina Beyincé. When Tina realized the Beyincé family was running out of male children, she wanted to preserve the family name. So she changed her last name slightly and gave it to her daughter as a first name.

Not all of her family was pleased. Tina's father said that other kids would pick on her because she has a last name for a first name. But Tina didn't think so.

Since Mathew and Tina were both very successful, the Knowles family lived in a six-bedroom house in a wealthy part of Houston called the Third Ward. Almost five years later, in 1986, her parents had another child. It was a girl they named Solange. Beyoncé grew up listening to the music her parents loved. This included African-American artists, such as Marvin Gaye, Barry White, Luther Vandross, and Michael Jackson.

From the beginning, Beyoncé loved music. She recalled her love of music in *Soul Survivors*, a book published in 2002. It is an autobiography of Beyoncé's first hit group, Destiny's Child. Beyoncé wrote: "My dad tells me that as a baby, I would go crazy whenever I heard music, and I tried to dance before I could even walk. He has the embarrassing videos to prove it!"

Beyoncé began her education at St. Mary's Elementary School in Houston. She was a quiet girl. She would rather stare at the floor than raise her hand to answer a question asked by the teacher. She was usually on her best behavior. If a student tried talking to her in class, she whispered to him or her to stop it. She did not want to get in trouble.

But she loved math and compared it to figuring out riddles. She felt good when she could help a student who had trouble with math. Still, her shyness took over when she was called to the chalkboard to write an answer to a problem in front of the class. She always got nervous.

One day when she came home from first grade, Beyoncé sat down at the kitchen table. Her mother was washing dishes. She asked Beyoncé what she had learned that day in school. Beyoncé answered that she learned a song. Her mother turned around and said she wanted to hear it. Beyoncé said in *Soul Survivors*, "I stood up to sing it for her just like my teacher had taught me. I'll never forget that feeling. I loved performing for my mom—it was a rush."

Beyoncé may have been shy at school, but she loved to sing and dance at home. Her parents noticed her energy and signed her up for dance class at school. Beyoncé's teacher, Sister Darlette Johnson, told her at age seven that she could sing as well as dance. She talked Beyoncé into performing in a local talent competition. Sister Darlette suggested that Beyoncé sing John Lennon's classic song "Imagine." It is a ballad about imagining the world as a place of peace, unity, and love. Beyoncé was the youngest of the performers. She remembers she was terrified. But Sister Darlette prodded and encouraged her. Beyoncé remembered, "I was terrified and I didn't wanna do it, and she's like, 'C'mon, baby, get out there.' I remember walking out and I was scared, but when the music started, I don't know what happened. I just . . . changed."[1]

She realized that she was almost a different person when in front of an audience. The shy schoolgirl afraid to speak out in class acted like a little superstar. Her parents couldn't believe that was their quiet daughter on stage singing in front of a crowd.

Her father later told *Billboard* magazine, "She got up on stage and when she was finished, she received a standing ovation. Her mother and I looked at each other and said, 'That can't be our Beyoncé. She's shy and quiet.'"

Beyoncé won the competition. Even more amazing, she had beaten contestants twice her age.

Beyoncé loved performing in front of an audience. But she also liked being a quiet girl and a tomboy. It was like there were two Beyoncés. Her parents recognized that their daughter could sing and dance better than other kids her age. They entered her into more Houston-area children's talent shows. She later told *Billboard* magazine, "I knew from . . . maybe around 8, that I got lost when I got onstage. It was like the most comfortable hour, a place where I could not be shy and not be aware of everything in my own world."[2]

In the contests, the kids were judged on their talent, appearance, and stage presence. She proved to be a natural talent and won several competitions. Her name was first mentioned in a newspaper, the *Houston Chronicle*, at age eight. She was nominated for a Houston-area performing arts award, the Sammy. Although she did not win, it was an accomplishment for a child so young to be nominated.

Around her ninth birthday, Beyoncé transferred to another school in Houston. It was called the Cynthia Ann Parker Elementary School. The Parker school is a magnet school, or a school for children who excel at certain abilities. The Parker School was for kids who were especially talented in music.

If Beyoncé was not rehearsing or attending classes at the Parker School, she was often in church. She has been very religious since her earliest years. At age nine, she worked with her church pastor helping people without homes or who could not afford to eat. She said in *Soul Survivors*, "I don't think I chose to be a singer—God put the talent in me." And with her beautiful voice, it was only natural that she was chosen to sing in the church choir. The church's gospel music was a huge influence on her. Later in her career, Beyoncé told *Scholastic Action*, "There's so much power in (gospel) music. I can't really describe it. There's so much happiness when you're singing."

One talent competition Beyoncé took part in at age nine was called the People's Workshop. It was one of the most popular talent shows in the Houston area. Celebrities often showed up to watch young, skilled children perform. Talent scouts also attended to discover the next big star. At the People's Workshop, Beyoncé met two people who would be important in her life. One was a girl her age named LaTavia Roberson. The other was a woman named Andretta Tillman, who was involved in the local music business. Her job was to take children with raw talent and turn them into polished performers. Tillman saw ability in Beyoncé and thought she had a future in the music business. She was putting together a girl group and asked Beyoncé to audition.

Tillman also asked LaTavia to audition. While Beyoncé's strong point was singing, LaTavia's best skill was dancing. Several dozen girls auditioned, and they formed an informal group that sang at banquets and small private or public events. At different times, the group performed with a handful of different girls. At that time, there were several singing and dancing boy bands, such as Backstreet Boys and N' Sync, who were big hit makers. They didn't play any instruments. Professional musicians did. Tillman thought there should be room in the music world for a band consisting just of girls singing and dancing. Since she thought it was time for girls, Tillman decided to call the group Girl's Tyme.

As a child, Beyoncé was nothing if not confident. On January 27, 1991, the Knowles family got ready to watch the Super Bowl. Music legend Whitney Houston sang the national anthem before the game. Not just any singer gets that big of an honor. Beyoncé was nine at the time. Her mother Tina told Suzanne Zuckerman of *People* magazine about that occasion. She said, "I remember her [Beyoncé] seeing Whitney Houston singing the national anthem and saying, 'I'm going to do that one day.'"

Tina reacted very matter-of-factly to her daughter's fantasy. She knew Beyoncé was talented but singing "The Star Spangled Banner" was a truly lofty goal. Tina simply answered to Beyoncé, "Okay. That sounds good."

Meanwhile, Girl's Tyme continued to practice and play local parties and venues. They still performed with different girls at different shows, but soon the group consisted mainly of five girls: Beyoncé, LaTavia, Tamar Davis, and Nikki and Nina Taylor.

Beyoncé's parents realized their daughter was serious about music. This wasn't merely a hobby to her. The girls would practice anywhere there was a vacant space, but one common location was Tina's beauty salon. It was one of Beyoncé's favorite places to hang out. She remembered that her mother would let her sweep cut hair off the floor. She also let them practice performing in front of salon customers. Beyoncé recalled, "Most of them were like, 'I just want to get a press and a curl. I don't want to hear this.' But we made them listen and then we insisted on money." The girls often used the money to go to a local theme park called AstroWorld.

Tina laughed when she thought back to those days, telling *Rolling Stone* magazine, "They used to go in and perform, and make the customers sit there. The customers couldn't leave, because they were locked under the dryers."

Around that time, Beyoncé met a friend of LaTavia named Kelindria Rowland, who was known by her nickname Kelly. LaTavia and Kelly had met in elementary school. Kelly loved singing as much as Beyoncé. She auditioned for Girl's Tyme as well and was accepted as another member of the group.

Unlike Beyoncé, Kelly was from a poor home. She was born in Atlanta, Georgia. Her parents divorced soon afterward. Kelly's mother, Doris, worked as a nanny for a family. The mother and daughter lived in the family's house. When the family moved from Atlanta to Houston, they took Doris and Kelly with them. When the family she worked with no longer needed Doris, she took several jobs with other families. Doris felt bad for Kelly having no stable home. Meanwhile, Kelly and Beyoncé hit it off right away.

Mathew and Tina also felt bad for Kelly having to move from one house to another. They offered Kelly the chance to move permanently into their home. Although the Knowles family never legally adopted Kelly, she more or less became part of the family. When Kelly's mother was not obligated to stay in another family's home, she also stayed with the Knowles family. Since Kelly never knew her father, she began referring to Mathew Knowles as her dad.

Beyoncé and Kelly got along as well as real sisters. They shared the same room. In their spare time, they played, sang, and watched television together. One television show they especially liked was *Showtime at the Apollo*. The Apollo Theater is the most famous showplace in the mostly African-American Harlem section of New York City. The program featured successful African-American acts performing onstage. Beyoncé and Kelly dreamed of singing in a famous theater someday.

However, they also spent time just being kids. Both girls loved watching the shows on the Disney Channel. They especially liked the *Mickey Mouse Club*, which was broadcast on the Disney Channel every weekday. Kelly remembered in *Soul Survivors*, "We were both the biggest Mickey Mouse fans, so our room was like the Mouse Museum. We had our Mickey Mouse sheets, our Mickey Mouse lamp, our Mickey Mouse alarm clock, Mickey Mouse everything—it was so cute."

Beyoncé went so far as to draw Mickey Mouse ears on the room rug. Kelly recalled one incident when Beyoncé was drawing mouse ears on the wall with a magic marker. Just then, Beyoncé's mother walked in the girls' room. She was not pleased. Buying furniture and sheets with Mickey Mouses on them was all right. But she would not stand for informal drawings of the famous mouse on the clean rug and ceiling. She ended Beyoncé's playful drawing career.

Meanwhile, Girl's Tyme was gelling as a six-member group. They went from playing at parties to bigger and more well-respected events and arenas. That included the Wortham Center, where the professional Houston Ballet and Houston Grand Opera played regularly. Although Mathew's career with Xerox was booming, he decided to spend some time promoting Girl's Tyme. Mathew started his own music production company. He called it Music World Entertainment (MWE). Mathew soon worked part-time alongside Andretta Tillman as the Girl's Tyme comanagers.

Beyoncé said to *Essence* magazine, "When my dad stopped working his full-time job to manage us, everybody thought he was crazy. But my mother stood by him. She said, 'I'm his wife and I have my business and I'm going to work extra hours.' If she hadn't made that sacrifice, I wouldn't be where I am."

Without a background in the music industry, Mathew felt he needed to educate himself. He signed up for a class about the music business at Houston Community College. But he said his experience working for a big corporation like Xerox gave him more knowledge than the class did. Through the years, he had learned how to deal with people with different personalities and opinions. He admitted that selling medical imaging supplies was no different than selling Beyoncé to important people in the music industry and potential fans. Mathew told *Rolling Stone* simply, "When you're a good salesperson, then you're a good salesperson."

Mathew worked hard behind the scenes to get Girl's Tyme as many gigs as possible. If they put on a great show at one event, Mathew's ability as a salesperson combined with audiences telling their friends would lead to more Girl's Tyme performances.

Word was really getting out about this talented six-girl singing and dancing ensemble. A Houston record producer named Alonzo Jackson offered to work with them. His offer was accepted. They were written up in an article in the *Houston Chronicle* in the summer of 1992. The headline read, "GIRLS TIME: OK guys, step aside. Six Houston preteens figure it's their turn for success in the music business." The author of the article compared them to the all-girl superstar group at the time, En Vogue.

Girl's Tyme spent their actual time singing the latest hits to a karaoke machine, practicing dance routines in their homes, trying on outfits that Tina Knowles made, and learning how to deal with reporters and interviewers from Beyoncé's father and Andretta Tillman.

Years later, Beyoncé told *Scholastic Action* magazine, "When I was younger, a lot of people were going to parties. I was focused in the studio. When other kids were out playing, I wanted to be inside writing songs and practicing dancing. You have to make sacrifices."

As word about this up-and-coming vocal group called Girl's Tyme spread through the music business, a professional producer name Arne Frager took an interest in them. Frager was no amateur. He had worked with superstar Mariah Carey in the past. Frager worked out of a studio in Sausalito, California. It is just across the Golden Gate Bridge from San Francisco. Frager's studio was called the Record Plant. He invited the group to work in his studio and brought them to California. There, they recorded their first demo records. Demo is short for demonstration. Demo records are not meant to be heard by the public. They are made for people in the music business. These professionally trained music experts listen to beginning artists on demo records. If they like them, they might have them record music to be released to the public.

When she was about twelve, Beyoncé met a boy she liked. His name was Lindell. However, Beyoncé's mother would not allow her to date until she was sixteen. So they talked on the phone, and he rode his bicycle across town to visit her. They really liked each other and hung out a lot together.

But Beyoncé's main interest was not boys. It was becoming a professional performer. Simply put, music was her passion. And her first huge opportunity was waiting.

Chapter 3

GOOD-BYE GIRL'S TYME

In the 1980s and early 1990s, there was a popular television series called *Star Search*. It was a talent competition much like *American Idol*. Girl's Tyme auditioned for *Star Search* and was picked to compete on the show. They had hoped a win on *Star Search* would be the first step toward a major recording contract and concerts across the country.

At the time they appeared on *Star Search*, there were six members of Girl's Tyme. Beyoncé, Kelly, and a girl named Ashley were the singers. LaTavia, Nina, and Nikki were background dancers and did not sing.

Girl's Tyme was mistakenly introduced on the show as "a hip-hop rapping" group. They were competing against the previous week's champion, a rock band from Detroit called Skeleton Crew.

The members of Girl's Tyme all wore similar costumes: jean shorts and satin jackets. The outfits were color matched in pairs. Two wore purple, two wore white, and two wore lime green. After performing, each group on *Star Search* was awarded in scores up to four points each. Skeleton Crew won all four out of four votes. Girl's Tyme won three out of four. The girls felt they had done their best, and they were stunned to lose.

When the announcer told the audience that Girl's Tyme had lost, the cameras focused on the members' faces. The girls acted professionally. They put on fake smiles for the cameras while inside they were crying.

Right afterward, they went backstage. Out of the cameras' view, they could be themselves. The whole group started crying. Beyoncé said in *Soul Survivors*, "We all went crazy from crying—a lot was riding on the performance."

That night at dinner, Beyoncé's parents tried to cheer her up. They told her not to quit. But it did not do much good. Beyoncé added, "We cried ourselves to sleep that night—my Mickey Mouse pillow was drenched—and we thought about what my parents had said. The next morning, we all woke up saying, 'Forget it. We don't have what it takes. We'll never get another shot at performing on TV.'"

At first, Kelly blamed the producers of *Star Search*. She said the producers had placed Girl's Tyme, who were all about eleven or twelve years old, against a rock band made up of men twice their age. The men of Skeleton Crew had many more years of performing experience. She said it was not a fair competition.

But a while after the show was finished, the girls watched the videotape of their performance over and over. Enough time had passed that their raw emotions were gone.

Beyoncé said in *Soul Survivors* that they began to realize they did not deserve to win. She said that was hard for the group to admit. But as they watched the tape again and again, "Each time our mistakes became more apparent. One girl's voice was off-key. Another girl would forget a step. Kelly would sit right in front of the TV and tap her finger on the screen: 'Oh, we messed up here, we messed up there. We gotta fix these things.' We needed some work. We were good for our age, but that's not good enough to make it in the real world. It's a good thing we did not win any sympathy votes—otherwise we might not have worked so hard to get where we are today."

Mathew helped heal the girls' pride and boost their spirits when he told them that *Star Search* producer, Al Masini, told him that some artists who had lost on the show went on to achieve tremendous musical success. Masini said in Daryl Easlea's book, *Crazy in Love: The Beyoncé Knowles Biography*, "For those who lose, something happens. They go back and rededicate themselves, reorganize and some of them go on to make it. For some reason, those who win, don't go on."

The girls of Girl's Tyme buckled down and made rules to improve their act. These included: rehearse every day, start working out, make up new routines, learn to sing a cappella (without musical instruments backing them up), and stop watching *Star Search*.

Beyoncé trained herself not to get angry when she made mistakes. She did allow herself to get sad but added that challenges forced the girls to mature. She confessed in *Soul Survivors*, "Personal growth takes someone to boo you offstage. Life is about taking missteps, tripping, falling, dusting yourself off, getting back up, and working harder to get yourself further than where you were in the first place."

So the six girls tried their hardest again to get a contract with a record company. While they concentrated on performing, Mathew continued to make the business decisions that affected them.

Yet record label after record label told them the same thing. There were too many girls in the group. Then Mathew Knowles decided the group should drop the dancers. Girl's Tyme would continue to perform and try to make it big time but only as a trio of Beyoncé, Kelly, and Ashley.

However, Ashley suddenly left the group. She did not want to take the risks involved in trying to make it in show business. She knew that for every artist that succeeds, hundreds don't make it and are never heard from again.

However, LaTavia, who had been a dancer, did want to stay in the group. LaTavia took singing lessons from the band's vocal coach, David Brewer. After training hard, she became one of the Girl's Tyme singers. Then Beyoncé's father, Mathew, had an idea. Instead of the members of Girl's Tyme being either singers or dancers, they should do both. Mathew also had a feeling that the group would work better as a quartet than a trio. They held auditions for a fourth member in Beyoncé's house. They chose LeToya Luckett, who Beyoncé knew from school. LeToya had experience signing in her church choir.

Mathew then took a bold step. He quit his job with Xerox and became the girls' full-time manager. He modeled himself after Joe Jackson, father of the Jackson 5. The Jackson 5 was a singing and dancing group of brothers from Gary, Indiana. They had several megahits in the late 1960s and early 1970s. After several years together, the five members embarked on solo careers. Of course, the most famous was Michael Jackson, who became a music legend. Another superstar, Janet Jackson, was a sibling in the same family. However, she was not part of the group.

Although Girl's Tyme did not consist of siblings, Mathew felt the same model would work for them. Joe Jackson was known for being a tough manager. Some people thought he was too tough, and he worked his kids too hard. His attitude was always a source of controversy. But Mathew planned to use his drive to get the best out of the girls, without being a taskmaster. He used his determination to get Girl's Tyme to succeed.

Beyoncé's mother was not happy about Mathew quitting his job. Her salon was doing well, but the family was used to living with both parents working full-time jobs. Now their family income would be cut in half.

Mathew's time at home was cut greatly too. The time he spent trying to make Girl's Tyme into a success was taking a toll on his and Tina's marriage. After fourteen years of marriage, Mathew and Tina separated around Christmas in 1994. That means they did not legally divorce, but they lived apart from each other. Tina took her two daughters and Kelly Rowland and moved to a much smaller house in Houston.

Tina later told *Essence* magazine's Kierna Mayo, "We lost our house shortly after my husband, Mathew, left his job to manage the girls under their first record deal. . . . Mathew would spend $5,000 of our money on a photo shoot, while I was working 16 hours a day to support us. I felt like the group was more important to him than his family. So we separated for six months."[1]

Although his marriage to Tina suffered, Mathew did not give up trying to sign the girls to a record contract. He got local theaters to book them or sign them up for performances as opening acts for famous musical artists doing shows in Houston. When they were not performing or in school, he made the group do one thing repeatedly: practice, practice, practice.

He also got back together with Tina. She said to Kierna Mayo, "We were miserable apart. We got back together and [said we] would never let money separate us again."

Word started getting around the local music scene that Girl's Tyme truly had talent. In 1995, when Beyoncé and most of the other girls were fourteen, they were invited to two separate auditions. One was held at the Houston Jewish Community Center.

The center had enough open space for musical acts to show producers how they could sing and dance. The night before the audition, the girls did something foolish. They stayed up late and went swimming at a friend's house.

The next day, they were tired. Beyoncé admits she has bad sinuses, and her nose was still clogged from the pool. In the audience were just two people: Mathew Knowles and a woman named Teresa LaBarbera Whites. She was a representative from Columbia Records, one of the most successful companies in music history. Beyoncé was scared to take the stage in front of her father and an important woman in the music business.

The audition was a disaster. Mathew halted their performance in the middle. He asked the girls if they had gone swimming the night before. The girls said they did. He gave them a tongue-lashing. He said they looked tired and sounded poorly. The girls took Mathew's complaint seriously. They agreed not to do something like that again.

Beyoncé was slowly becoming the group's leader. Tina thinks it is because she has so much drive. When they were about fifteen, Tina treated the girls to a concert given by Janet Jackson. Tina told writer Mark Healy of *Marie Claire* magazine, "The others [group members] were like, 'That was great' but Beyoncé was already pulling it apart, trying to figure out what made it good. She said, 'One day I want to have a concert like that.'"[2]

Mathew continued to use his strong sales skills and determination to get the girls more auditions and appearances. He arranged to have Girl's Tyme perform at Houston's Black Expo.

Numerous other performers looking for a big break took the stage. Also in attendance were artist and repertoire (A&R) representatives from record labels. A&R reps are basically talent scouts. They look for new artists with talent, energy, and ambition to sign for their record labels. Once they sign musicians or singers, A&R reps help them learn the ins and outs of the business. They also assist by setting up recording sessions or suggesting songs for them to record.

A&R reps from Elektra Records showed interest in Girl's Tyme. A representative from Elektra told Girl's Tyme they were "very talented." But after Columbia Records heard their second audition, the label became seriously interested in signing them too.

It is a musician's dream to have two record labels interested in signing you. However, the girls were only fourteen and not mature enough to make such an important decision. So Mathew made the decision. He chose Elektra Records. In *Soul Survivors*, Beyoncé said she does not know why her father picked Elektra over Columbia. She feels it was mainly a business decision. Perhaps Elektra offered them more money. Anyway, she and her singing partners did not concern themselves with the business aspect of the recording deal. They were interested in making the best music they could.

Daryl Simmons, a production partner with Elektra, ran a business called Silent Partner Productions. Simmons had been a musician before he decided to work in the business end of the music industry. Over the years, he has worked behind the scenes on recordings by music stars, such as Aretha Franklin, Whitney Houston, Bobby Brown, Toni Braxton, and Aaliyah. Simmons believed that Beyoncé had the most natural talent of the group. So he wanted to make sure her vocals were dominant on any records they made. Tina took breaks from her beauty salon to help design the girls' hair. She became their personal assistant. It was Tina who first put blonde highlights in Beyoncé's hair.

There was one catch about working with Elektra and Silent Partner Productions. They were based in Atlanta, about eight hundred miles away from Houston and the group's family and friends. Moving to a new city would be a difficult step. But it was also exciting to live in a different city.

So they moved from Houston to Atlanta. LaTavia's mother moved with them, so there would be an adult to watch over them. The other girls' families flew to Atlanta when they could to visit their daughters. They spent their days split between lessons with a private tutor and time in the recording studio. At night, they all slept in the basement of Simmons's assistant's house. It was cramped, but the girls liked being independent and really felt they had grown up a lot because of the big move. They were also paid a little money every day, called a per diem. It is similar to an allowance. They loved shopping on weekends in Atlanta's biggest malls.

But what seemed like a dream opportunity started to sputter. Girl's Tyme made a few recordings, but the members felt Elektra Records' producers were not making a great effort to promote them. To promote a musician, or any kind of entertainer, means trying to get them on television shows, radio stations, or on the Internet. They could send the group as opening acts for more famous artists' tours. But Girl's Tyme just lingered at Elektra for months.

Kelly remembered that despite their youth, the girls saw it was clear that Elektra was doing nothing to help further their careers. After a mere eight months, they received a letter in the mail from the president of Elektra. It said that the record label was dropping them. According to *Essence* magazine, the letter read that the group was "too young and underdeveloped."

Kelly surmised in *Soul Survivors*, "Initially they seemed excited, but I guess they had too much other stuff going on, other established artists who were selling very well at the time." The girls' reactions were the same as when they lost on *Star Search*. They cried and felt hopeless. They left Atlanta to move back home to Houston.

It was Mathew who came through for them again. He gave them a pep talk. He said another label would want them even if Elektra didn't. He told them to use the Elektra rejection as motivation to work harder and make their act a little tighter. Mathew said that he was not going to give up, so they should not either.

As part of their growth, the girls of Girl's Tyme decided they needed a new image. They felt the name Girl's Tyme seemed too juvenile. And by now, the name reeked of failure to the quartet. So they considered new names such as Somethin' Fresh, Cliché, Borderline, and the Dolls. They finally settled on Destiny.

Tina liked the name, as it is a common theme in the Book of Isaiah in the Bible. Mathew added the word *child* to indicate the girls might be teens, but they would grow—along with their talent. So they would not let their skills get rusty, the group, now officially known as Destiny's Child, continued singing at local gigs.

Mathew once again used his business know-how and his way with people to take the group a step forward. In 1995, he called Teresa LaBarbera Whites from Columbia Records. Whites was the woman who had heard the group's poor audition the day after they went swimming. Mathew convinced Whites to give another audition to the same group with a different name. She had been interested in signing them a few years ago and still knew in her heart that they had natural talent.

Whites flew them to Columbia's main office in New York City. Destiny's Child was taken to a tiny conference room. It was filled with couches. On the couches were several of Columbia's production and A&R people. Beyoncé remembered being nervous and scared as she and the other members were about to sing in front of important people. To make things more nerve-wracking, there were no microphones. And there was not enough room for instruments. Destiny's Child was forced to audition a cappella.

They sang two songs. One was a moody ballad titled "Ain't No Sunshine." It was a hit by rhythm-and-blues singer Bill Withers in 1971. The other was a tune called "Are You Ready?" that Destiny's Child had developed on their own.

They returned home to Houston and waited to hear back from Whites and the other people at Columbia. It was not easy being patient. But the girls waited. And waited. And waited—over a period of several weeks. They were hoping that any day a letter from Columbia would arrive in the mail. And one day, it finally did.

Chapter 4

YES, YES, YES

Mathew and Tina saw a letter with the return address of Columbia Records. They opened it to discover the best news: Columbia Records was officially offering Destiny's Child a recording contract.

Both Tina and Mathew thought it would be fun to play a joke on the girls. They put the contract in an envelope from a regional restaurant chain called Luby's Cafeteria. The Knowles family usually ate there for lunch after church. Tina and the group were at her beauty salon when Mathew and Tina handed them the envelope with "Luby's" printed on it.

Beyoncé and the girls thought the envelope contained a gift certificate to Luby's. Beyoncé remembered in *Soul Survivors*, "When we saw it was a recording contract, we started screaming and crying right in the middle of the salon. The ladies with their heads under the dryers looked at us like we were crazy, because they couldn't hear what all the yelling was about. We ran all around the shop, jumping up and down, holding our contract in the air for all the customers to see."

Columbia Records has been around since 1887 and has released music from some of the most legendary artists in the business. The list includes Frank Sinatra, Bob Dylan, Duke Ellington, Bruce Springsteen, Michael Jackson, and Mariah Carey.

Unlike the disaster with Elektra Records, Columbia really wanted to work with the quartet. Neither side wasted any time. In early 1996, the group signed a contract with Columbia Records. Beyoncé was just fifteen. At the same time, Destiny's Child signed another contract. This was with Mathew. That contract made him their full-time manager.

At first, LeToya Luckett's and LaTavia Roberson's parents were uneasy to give Mathew Knowles so much control over their daughters' musical careers.

Andretta Tillman would still work with them as a comanager, but Mathew would be the top boss. He convinced Luckett's and Roberson's parents that he had been with the girls since day one. He knew their ups and downs and had watched them mature from preteens to adolescents. He felt he was so familiar with them that it would be foolish to put their careers in the hands of someone unfamiliar with the group.

Right away, Destiny's Child began work on their first album. At the same time, they tried to live the lives of average teenagers. That was nearly impossible. Yet believe it or not, Beyoncé was still dating her first boyfriend, Lindell. That was when she had leisure time, which was not very often.

The girls still attended public school, even as they were working on their album. However, that proved to be difficult. They attended school through the first semester of ninth grade. But the time and energy they had to spend in the recording studio distracted them from their studies. They finally left public school early in 1997. Instead of having traditional classroom educations, they were given private tutors. The learning sessions were intense and there were no breaks. When their lessons were over, they went right to the recording studio. In *Soul Survivors*, Kelly said, "But for us, it was just about learning as much as possible as quickly as possible."

They actually had their first recording released before they had finished their album. It was one song on the sound track of the smash action-adventure movie *Men in Black*. The movie starred Will Smith and Tommy Lee Jones. Destiny's Child contributed a ballad titled "Killing Time." The album reached number one for a week on the top-selling albums chart on *Billboard* magazine. So millions of people who bought the *Men in Black* sound track heard the first sounds of the formerly unknown quartet from Houston, Texas.

Things were progressing well: 1996 turned into 1997 and they were still developing their first album. But while working on the album, they received some tragic news. Comanager Andretta Tillman, who had been with the girls from the beginning, died from a condition called lupus. Lupus occurs when a person's immune system attacks his or her own tissues and organs.

The girls were heartbroken. They made sure they would never forget what Tillman had done for them.

Destiny's Child continued working on their first album for the rest of 1997. As is common in the recording industry, Columbia released the first single from their debut album before the album was released. If listeners like the new single, they will be interested in hearing what the rest of the album sounds like.

So in the fall of 1997, they made a slow, soulful song titled "No, No, No." Teresa LaBarbera Whites and others at Columbia liked it but did not think it was strong enough to grab listeners' attention as a first single. So they grabbed another Columbia artist, Wyclef Jean, to add his input. Jean had been with a hip-hop group called the Fugees, short for "refugees," and was hot at that time. He told the group to speed up the tempo. He also added a rap interlude. His version of Destiny's Child's first single was merely called "No, No, No Part 2." The record was credited to Destiny's Child featuring Wyclef Jean. In early 1998, the song reached number three on *Billboard's* top records chart.

Beyoncé remembered when she first heard her song on the radio. It was a weekday afternoon, and she was driving the Ford Explorer her parents had given her as a sixteenth birthday present. Kelly was a passenger, and they had the radio on. They pulled up to the neighborhood high school to pick up Beyoncé's sister, Solange. Suddenly, "No, No, No Part 2" came on the radio. She and Kelly turned up the volume as high as possible. They got out of the car and ran around singing along. Solange walked up to the car and thought Beyoncé and Kelly were acting crazy. She asked what was wrong with them.

As soon as Solange approached the car and heard what song was being played, she dropped her books and ran around the car with them. Beyoncé has never forgotten that moment. She remembered, "It was a really cool experience."

Soon it was time for the album to be released. It came out in February 1998. Kelly Rowland explained that the singers took two years to work on it because they wanted it to be the best possible album they could make.

For an established band, the success of the album, *Destiny's Child*, might have been disappointing. It made *Billboard* magazine's weekly top 100 list of album sales but never got higher than number 67. However, it did go on to sell more than 3 million copies. For a first album, it was an achievement, especially for a group of teenagers. The girls were delighted. Mathew continued to do his best to get publicity for the singers. One early fan of the group was superstar Whitney Houston. She invited the teens to perform at her thirty-fifth birthday celebration in August 1998. They did not want to miss that chance.

They bought matching outfits and came dressed as a group. But they were the only guests dressed that way. All the other guests came dressed in individual outfits. People kept telling Destiny's Child that they looked like the Supremes, one of the best-known and most-loved girl singing groups in music history. Since music writers were constantly comparing Destiny's Child to the Supremes, that was the last thing Beyoncé wanted to hear. She and the other girls in Destiny's Child admired the Supremes, but they weren't the Supremes. They were their own group: Destiny's Child.

They might have been socializing with the cream of the music world, but underneath it all, they were still schoolgirls from Houston. They had to take lessons from their tutors. Between studying and working in the studio, they did not have much time for social lives. However, Beyoncé's longtime boyfriend, Lindell Locke, invited her to his senior prom. So in a very short time, Beyoncé went from celebrating with Whitney Houston to going to a high school prom. What sticks out in her mind is that since the prom was at his school—and he was two years older than her—she did not know any of the other students. And although she was a famous recording star, Beyoncé's parents gave her a curfew. She remembers having to be home early that night.

With the momentum they had from their first album, Destiny's Child got busy on a second one. Rowland said they studied their first album—what they thought worked and what did not work. Columbia producer Whites again worked closely with them.

Whites told them about another producer who would be perfect to work with the group. His real name was Kevin Briggs, but his stage name was She'kspere. He wrote songs with his girlfriend, Kandi Burrus, a singer with an Atlanta-based R&B band called Xscape. Xscape had nine top-forty hits between 1993 and 2000. She'kspere also produced for Xscape. At the same time, he was also working with another famous all-girl R&B group, TLC. She'kspere was making a name for himself as a top R&B producer.

She'kspere and Burrus went over song ideas with Destiny's Child. They suggested arrangements, melodies, and lyrics. The couple wound up being involved in some way with five songs on the second album. A total of sixteen producers worked with the girls on the new album, but it was truly She'kspere's and Burrus's input that gave the record its direction—a punchy and soulful R&B sound. It was reminiscent of classic R&B of the 1970s.

With experience and top guidance behind them, Destiny's Child finished their second album in much less time than it took to produce the first. It was released July 27, 1999, about a year and a half after their first one. The girls chose a biblical verse for the album name: *The Writing's on the Wall.* It is found in the book of Daniel in the Old Testament. The actual writing, as it was mentioned in the Bible, referred to an engraving on a wall that predicted the downfall of the mighty Babylonian empire.

The girls were growing up. In 1999, each was either eighteen or about to turn eighteen. So it is natural that *The Writing's on the Wall* features the girls singing more mature songs. They got away from simple love songs and moved more toward songs with deeper themes about relationships between men and women. After spending so much time in her mother's beauty salon, Beyoncé noticed topics that older women tend to talk about while getting their hair done. She used those conversations to inspire her in writing lyrics alongside the other Destiny's Child members.

The first song to be released from *The Writing's on the Wall* was titled "Bills, Bills, Bills." It was a tough take on men who used women for their money, such as using all the gas in their cars and not refilling the tanks or recklessly using the women's credit cards. The official video was shot in a reproduced hair salon with women under hair dryers. The members of Destiny's Child played hairdressers listening to and talking to the customers as they styled their hair.

"Bills, Bills, Bills" reached number one for one week on the Billboard Hot 100 singles chart—the group's first number one song. But there was an even bigger hit on the album. It is titled "Say My Name" and was number one for three weeks.

The girls in the group also had another fine accomplishment to savor in 2000. Through work with their tutors, they earned enough credits, or passed enough courses, to receive high school diplomas. So even though they had not attended a traditional high school, they were officially high school graduates.

But while Destiny's Child seemed like one happy group of singing friends on the outside, things were darker behind their performances. LeToya and LaTavia had been growing resentful of Beyoncé and Kelly. LeToya and LaTavia believed they were being shoved into the background while Beyoncé and Kelly were becoming the stars of the group. They thought it had nothing to do with talent. They felt it was because manager Mathew Knowles was giving his daughter special treatment. They also thought the special treatment extended to Kelly because she was closer to Mathew than they were. So LeToya, LaTavia, and their parents fired Mathew as their manager. They wanted their own manager who they thought would treat them as equals to Beyoncé and Kelly.

The quartet tried to work out their problems. They tried everything from rotating hotel rooms to getting counseling from their church pastor. Nothing worked. In *Soul Survivors*, Beyoncé said LeToya and LaTavia were simply jealous. Beyoncé also said that LeToya and LaTavia wanted the group to seem less squeaky-clean. Beyoncé and her father wanted Destiny's Child to maintain its wholesome Christian image.

Despite the pressures, LeToya and LaTavia still planned to join Beyoncé and Kelly to make the video for the song "Say My Name." So they were stunned to realize they were removed from the band. Two new girls, Michelle Williams and Farrah Franklin, replaced LeToya and LaTavia in the video. Michelle had been a professional backup singer for R&B performer Monica. Farrah had danced with Destiny's Child in the "Bills, Bills, Bills" video.

LeToya and LaTavia did not take this sitting down. They filed a lawsuit against Mathew, Beyoncé, and Kelly. A lawsuit meant that the girls thought they were treated unfairly according to their contract. Breaking a contract is against the law. They felt they had been forced out of the group, and Mathew owed them money. They even said that Mathew was abusive toward them.

Of course, once the gossip media realized two of the Destiny's Child girls had been fired, they could not get enough of the sensational story. Each reporter the girls spoke with wanted to hear something nasty about the breakup. All Beyoncé said was that LeToya and LaTavia left due to creative differences. That was partly true, because LeToya and LaTavia wanted to take the group in a different direction than Beyoncé and Kelly.

Finally, Kelly snapped. She could not hold back any longer. According to the book *Crazy in Love*, Kelly told a reporter that LeToya and LaTavia "were very negative and jealous." She continued, "They weren't able to do leads by themselves. We went to voice lessons because we wanted strong vocals. They wouldn't do that. They'd just show up when it was time to make money."

The music and gossip media loved it. It was as if Destiny's Child had its own soap opera. Before this mess, Destiny's Child was seen as a wholesome group with no controversies. There were articles written about them, but they were always positive. To many readers, that did not make them as interesting as when there is dramatic news to report. After the departure of LaTavia and LeToya, the media gave much more newspaper and magazine space and airtime to the growing saga of Destiny's Child. The silver lining was that the more Destiny's Child was in the news, the more people heard about them. And the more people heard about them, the more they wanted to buy their music.

But there was a serious downside. People started Web sites bashing Beyoncé and Destiny's Child. The sites had titles such as "Down With Destiny" and

"Top Reasons Why I Hate Beyoncé." The list included: "1. Conceited. 2. Kicked LaTavia and LeToya out . . . 5. 2-faced . . . 7. Daddy's Little Girl."[1] The haters did not limit their criticism to the Internet. They bashed her in person. Tina Knowles told Michael Hall of *Texas Monthly* magazine, "A lot of people dumped everything on Beyoncé. They would say things to her in airports—rude, evil things."

The constant backbiting and sniping took a toll on Beyoncé. She began suffering from severe depression. The depression was so strong that it affected Beyoncé's daily life. She told writer Danyel Smith for *Teen People* magazine, "For a month I stayed in bed. I was sad, hurt, on the verge of a nervous breakdown. I was thinking, 'Is all this worth it?' But I realized it's dumb to dwell on negativity."[2]

Then, in the summer of 2000, another bombshell hit. On July 17, the group was about to depart on a concert tour of Australia. Just before they were scheduled to leave, Farrah Franklin announced she did not want to go with them. Farrah told the media she left because the group members did not get along. But Michelle Williams told *Rolling Stone* magazine that Farrah could not take the stress that went with being in a hit musical group.

There is constant traveling from one city to another to do shows. Beyoncé told *Teen People* magazine that the hardest parts of being in Destiny's Child were "being tired" and "having to perform when you're sick or having a bad day."

There are press conferences, where the band members answer questions from the media. Much of the time, they have to answer the same questions repeatedly with identical answers. It can be tedious. According to Michelle, Farrah was burned out after five months and quit.

On July 17, Destiny's Child did leave for their concert tour of Australia—as a trio: Beyoncé, Kelly, and Michelle. They toured the rest of the year that way in the United States as well. The controversy may have made the girls struggle with their emotions, but it did keep them in the news.

One night, Beyoncé had an argument with her boyfriend, Lindel. She was also tired of the sniping between the group's members. So she went into a recording studio by herself and recorded a song she wrote titled "Independent Women, Part I." The point of the song was women shouldn't have to rely on men for their happiness.

She played it for her father and music executives at Columbia Records. The staff at Columbia thought it would be perfect for the sound track of a new movie Columbia studios (part of the same company) was making. It was titled *Charlie's Angels*, based on a television series that ran in the 1970s. It was a crime show, and the show's plot involved three glamorous women who solve crimes. While audiences thought it was unrealistic—the women never seemed to have a hair out of place even when they were chasing criminals—it was a hit. A lot of its audience saw it as a fun show and did not take it seriously. They saw it as light entertainment.

The people at Columbia thought some lyrics had to be changed to work better with the movie's theme. Beyoncé remembered, "So we went back in the studio. I went in with the girls and changed some of the words and made it fit the movie. It ended up being the single [from the movie] and it turned out to be our biggest song." The movie made money for the studio, although critics' reviews were mixed. But the song held the number one spot on the Billboard Top 100 for eleven weeks in late 2000.

The year ended on a high note. LeToya and LaTavia met with Beyoncé, and they all decided to stop publicly insulting each other. They had enough bad publicity by then. The insults were becoming stressful and a distraction. LeToya and LaTavia dropped their lawsuit against Beyoncé and Kelly. But they did not drop the lawsuit against Mathew.

For Destiny's Child, the new year kicked off with a splash. Early in 2001, "Say My Name" was nominated for two Grammy Awards. Members of the National Academy of Recording Arts and Sciences choose the Grammy Awards. They include performers as well as producers and those who work behind the scenes. Although there are many award shows that honor musical artists, the Grammys are the oldest and most revered. "Say My Name" was nominated in the categories of Best R&B Song and Best R&B Performance by a Duo or Group With Vocals. It won both awards! Winning two Grammys proved that Destiny's Child was a mainstream success.

They were now famous enough to be asked to perform at President George W. Bush's inauguration ceremonies. The new president, like the group, hailed from Texas. But when asked, Beyoncé refused to answer questions about her political views.

Soon, there was something beyond the world of music waiting for Beyoncé.

Chapter 5

BEYONCÉ ON THE BIG SCREEN

Producers at the cable television network MTV were planning to make a movie called *Carmen: A Hip Hopera*. It was based on one of the world's most famous operas: *Carmen* by George Bizet. *Carmen*, set in Spain, first premiered in France in 1875. The title character is a devious woman. She seduces a soldier who leaves his girlfriend for her. She then breaks up with the soldier to be with a glamorous bullfighter. It has been filmed, performed, and adapted for different media over the years.

Carmen: A Hip Hopera was updated to take place in a present-day American inner city. In this adaptation, Carmen is an African-American woman who seduces a police officer (played by Mekhi Phifer). Then she leaves him for a rapper named Blaze, played by Casey Lee. The people at MTV were familiar with Destiny's Child's music videos. They thought Beyoncé had a natural gift for acting. They wanted her to play the lead role in this updated version of *Carmen*.

The movie was made for television. At first, Beyoncé had concerns about playing the part of Carmen. Beyoncé's personality was completely opposite of the character. She considered it and, after some time, decided to take the role. She came to the conclusion that she was not being herself. She was an actor playing a character. If she was going to act, she would have to take roles out of her comfort zone.

Carmen: A Hip Hopera took about three months to shoot. The experience filming the project was both a growing and learning experience for Beyoncé, now twenty years old. She would have to move to Los Angeles for those three months. That meant being away from her friends and family. She said in *Soul Survivors* in 2002, "I missed my girls while I was on the set of *Carmen*. I may have been lonely at first, but I tried to look at that as a challenge. It was refreshing to have to go out of my way to get to know other people and become more social. I'm not a loner, but at the same time, I'm not what you would call a social butterfly. I haven't had the time to be exposed to a lot of people outside of my family and my group."

So Beyoncé made new friends as she worked on the movie. She further said in *Soul Survivors*, "I had to work with different makeup artists, wardrobe stylists, a director, a producer and an entire cast. We became very close." Beyoncé could relax and be herself when taking a break from filming. When she was filming a scene, she found herself being forced to talk to directors and defend her concerns. "So it was way more than a movie for me," she told *Rolling Stone* magazine.

Some critics liked the movie. Just as many did not. It was basically a 50-50 split among critics on the quality of *Carmen: A Hip Hopera*. However, there was general agreement that Beyoncé had a future as an actress. Some singers make movies, and they are in over their heads. Beyoncé is not one of them.

And something bigger was coming—not just for Beyoncé but for all the members of Destiny's Child. Their new album, *Survivor*, was released on May 1, 2001. It took off like a rocket. The album entered *Billboard* magazine's top 200 albums chart at number one. Four singles were released from the album, including "Independent Women." One of the singles,

"Survivor," won the group another Grammy Award for Best R&B Vocal by a Duo or Group. But the biggest hit on the album was "Bootylicious." In August, the song reached number one on *Billboard*'s singles chart, and it stayed at the top spot for two weeks.

"Bootylicious" is a slang term describing an attractive, full-figured woman. Beyoncé told music writer Fred Bronson, "It was a song of empowerment for people who didn't look like everyone in the magazines. They had a little meat on their bones, a little jelly. People still misunderstand the song. If someone says you need to lose weight or you don't look a certain way, you tell them you're too bootylicious for them." In other words, if a woman does not look like a fashion model, she should still feel good about herself. The music video that went with the song highlighted the three members. After all, they were the singers. But it also showed plus-sized women dancing to the song.

Because of the content of their first two albums, Destiny's Child had an image of being conservative and regular churchgoers. *Survivor* had more suggestive songs, such as "Bootylicious," than their first two albums. It was a way for the group to show their audiences that they were not teenage girls anymore. They had grown up. On stage and in their videos, they wore tight dresses and revealing clothing. Did dressing like that make them hypocrites since they stressed how the church is so important in their lives?

Beyoncé told *Newsweek* magazine, "It's entertainment, and I believe God is okay with that." Indeed, *Survivor* includes a medley of gospel songs that would be sung in church. The medley was dedicated to Andretta Tillman.

Then, a national catastrophe took place that would make gossip and clothing choices seem meaningless. On September 11, 2001, terrorists from an extremist Muslim group called Al-Qaeda attacked well-known landmarks in the United States. They hijacked commercial jetliners and flew them into the two towering office buildings of the World Trade Center in New York City. They flew another into the Pentagon building just outside Washington, D. C. The Pentagon is the official headquarters of the United States Defense Department. A fourth airplane crashed into a Pennsylvania field when passengers fought back against the hijackers. It is thought that the hijackers planned to fly it into either the White House or the U. S. Capitol building.

Almost three thousand innocent people were killed in the attacks. The death toll included hundreds of firefighters and paramedics who had gone into the World Trade Center to rescue people. Americans and most people around the world were shocked and sickened by this crime. Almost immediately, people gave money or held benefits to raise money for the victims' families. Musicians performed benefit concerts, and Destiny's Child did its part.

They played at the headliner-filled "The Concert for New York City" on October 20, 2001. Other guest performers included music legends David Bowie, Mick Jagger, Billy Joel, the Who, Elton John, and hip-hop all-star Jay-Z. It was there that Beyoncé met Jay-Z for the first time. Destiny's Child performed their single "Emotion," a ballad that dates back to the disco era of the mid- and late-1970s. They also sang a gospel medley. The next night, they made the trip to Washington to do a similar show. Mathew convinced them to sing "Survivor," which had much meaning for all of America at that time.

Beyoncé said in *Soul Survivors*, "In D. C. we sang 'Survivor,' which we weren't going to do, because we hadn't performed it in forever. We didn't have our backup dancers and we were used to doing it as the tour version. But my dad said, 'You know how many people out there feel like survivors and need to hear that song?'"

She added, "And we did it. It was the best crowd response and energy ever for that song because it was so real and so many people felt it."

Because of the terrorist attacks, flight schedules were erratic during the next several weeks. So Destiny's Child canceled a tour they were to do in Europe. However, they did release a Christmas album that month. It was titled *8 Days of Christmas*. Their version of the legendary carol "The Little Drummer Boy" featured an extra Knowles voice. Little sister Solange sang along with the group.

Then on March 12, 2002, they released an album consisting of remixes of their hit songs from their first four years. It was titled simply *This Is the Remix* and was highlighted with guest appearances by Wyclef Jean and Da Brat. Perhaps not surprisingly, the release of *This Is the Remix* led to new lawsuits filed by former Destiny's Child members LeToya Luckett and LaTavia Roberson. They specifically objected to the remix of "Survivor," which included the line, "You thought I wouldn't sell without you—sold nine million." Luckett and Roberson took it as a personal insult. They also said it was a violation of one of their previous agreements from the earlier lawsuit—that no member would make public comments insulting another person from the group. Like the first lawsuit, this was settled out of court too.

That year, the three members of Destiny's Child published their book, *Soul Survivors: The Official Autobiography of Destiny's Child*. It was written with the help of a professional writer and editor named James Patrick Herman. It consists mainly of direct quotes from the three members about everything from their childhoods to their religious views to what it feels like to rehearse and then take the stage. Its release also marked a major change in the group's career. Around the time the book came out, they agreed to take a break from singing as a group. They wanted to test their creativity as solo artists. The group split on good terms, however, and they swore they would be back again in just a few years singing as Destiny's Child.

Beyoncé's first project as a solo artist was not another album. It was making another movie. She took her mother to an audition for a role in a comedy, which would be called *Austin Powers in Goldmember*. It was the third movie in comedian Mike Myers's Austin Powers series. They were all parodies, or comic takeoffs, on the many secret agent movies of the 1960s. The character of Austin Powers was an international spy.

Beyoncé was trying out for the part of Foxxy Cleopatra. That character was a parody of crime-fighting female African-American heroes from action-adventure movies in the 1970s. They were known for being attractive and for their abilities to keep up with male spies. The character's name was a combination of Foxy Brown and Cleopatra Jones, two real characters from different movies in this genre.

Beyoncé said that she felt uneasy during the audition. She was not familiar with the movie industry terminology and that made her uncomfortable. She did not want to show her lack of knowledge on this subject. She said in *Soul Survivors,* "I was scared that I was going to say the wrong thing and ruin it, so I thought it would be best if I listened and didn't say much. My mom did all the talking—fortunately, she's a real charmer, and she did everything but read my lines for me!"

Beyoncé also did not like the audition setting. It took place in a stuffy office with overly bright lights. She stated that it was hard to get into the wild character of Foxxy Cleopatra in such a sterile setting. So she was surprised when her agent called her shortly after the audition to tell her she got the part.

During the filming, she and Myers got along very well. She learned a lot from him about successfully doing comedy. Despite the fact that she had acted in *Carmen,* she still did not feel confident as an actress. She further noted that making a movie is not for lazy people. For one thing, she had to work out with a physical trainer and watch everything she ate. It was not easy memorizing many lines of dialogue. There are a lot more words in a screenplay than in a song.

And having to say them with the right amount of expression while doing action scenes, such as kicking down a door, is a tough feat.

Austin Powers in Goldmember received mixed reviews from the critics. Some thought it was too vulgar, and the jokes were too juvenile. A few said the Austin Powers movies had run their course. Others simply thought it was funny despite the low level of humor. Regardless, the movie was a financial success. According to Internet Movie Database (IMDB), it cost about $63 million to make and earned over $213 million.

Thanks to the movie, even people who do not buy records now knew Beyoncé. Businesses wanted her to do advertisements for their products. They felt she had a positive image and was a good role model. One such company was Pro-Line hair products, based in her hometown of Houston. Another was fashionable Candie's Shoes. However, the biggest company to sign Beyoncé was Pepsi Cola. An all-American soft drink that has been around for ages, Pepsi selected Beyoncé to replace Britney Spears as its spokesperson.

By this time, her busy schedule caused her to end her longtime relationship with Lindell. Beyoncé stated to *Rolling Stone* magazine's Jangee Dunn, "We still talk all the time. We're like childhood friends."

She went back in the recording studio in 2002 and created a new song with Jay-Z, the rapper she had met at the Concert for New York City a year earlier. The credit for the song, titled "'03 Bonnie & Clyde," officially read, "Jay-Z featuring Beyoncé." The song title referred to a 1967 movie called *Bonnie and Clyde*. It was based on the lives of two bank robbers in the 1930s. The song reached number four on the Billboard Top 100 chart. More importantly to Beyoncé, it marked the start of a romantic relationship between the two. Jay-Z, whose real name is Shawn Carter, was born and raised in a tough section of Brooklyn, New York. His upbringing was as different from Beyoncé's as one can imagine. But together, they hit it off as a couple.

If people did not know Beyoncé in the beginning of 2003, they certainly knew her by the end of the year. Her first solo album, *Dangerously in Love*, was released on June 22. Around the same time, another movie costarring Beyoncé was released—*The Fighting Temptations*.

Dangerously in Love debuted at number one on *Billboard*'s top albums chart. It included a mixture of ballads and up-tempo rhythm-and-blues numbers. Beyoncé had a hand in writing all but three of the fifteen songs on the album. The first single from the album, "Crazy in Love," was a funky number with a brassy horn section and featured her boyfriend, Jay-Z, doing a rap interlude.

Beyoncé told writer Dennis Hensley, "The song talks about how, when you're falling in love, you do things that are out of character and you don't really care because you're just open. The song came from me actually looking crazy one day in the studio." It became a monster hit, staying at number one on the Billboard Hot 100 singles chart for eight weeks. It also became one of the songs Beyoncé would become most identified with. The album went on to win five Grammy Awards.

Beyoncé took a break from her budding solo career to get together with Kelly and Michelle to perform at one concert as Destiny's Child in July 2003. It took place in Montego Bay, Jamaica, at a music festival. They talked about missing each other and felt they should work as a group again. So they made plans to do so in the future.

While people were listening to Beyoncé on their radios that summer, many of her fans also went to the movies to see the comedy-drama *The Fighting Temptations*. The movie tells the story of a man in the advertising business in New York City. He learns that his great aunt has left him a huge inheritance. But to collect it, he must become the director of the gospel choir in his great aunt's church in the small Southern town where he grew up. Since the choir is not very good, he recruits a wide range of people to become new choir members. Beyoncé plays Lilly, his former girlfriend that he left back home. Her role calls for her to sing but also act in a wide variety of scenes.

Beyoncé was excited about taking the role. She told *Jet* magazine, "In the script, Lilly is very earthy. I saw a lot of comedic and dramatic opportunities in playing this character, and I knew I'd have a lot of fun with it. I was also drawn to the script as a whole. It's so full of attitude and energy."

According to the Internet Movie Database, *The Fighting Temptations* was made for about $15 million. It earned back about $30 million. The reviews were mixed. Critic Mick LaSalle of the *San Francisco Chronicle* liked the movie overall. He loved the music and wrote: "[Beyoncé] Knowles is the main musical attraction of the film."[1]

On the other hand, online movie critic James Berardinelli was not so complimentary. He wrote: "The casting of Beyoncé Knowles is emblematic of the film's fatal flaw. Knowles shines when she is performing as a singer, whether it's solo or as a member of the choir. As an actress, however, she is flat and unconvincing."

Later that summer, another cut from *Dangerously in Love* was released. It is titled "Baby Boy," and it is about her infatuation with a boy. This time, the guest performer was rapper Sean Paul. It was another success and stayed at number one on the Billboard Hot 100 chart for nine weeks.

Meanwhile, Beyoncé and Jay-Z continued to see each other. They never publicly announced their relationship, but there were rumors that they were a couple.

Beyoncé feels that her personal life should remain private. She confided, "I never talked about relationships. Even in school I never did. I only talk about them in my songwriting; otherwise things get too messy. It has worked because now nobody expects me to talk about them."[2]

Audiences did get to see the celebrity couple of Beyoncé and Jay-Z in public on August 28, 2003. They performed together at the MTV Music Awards. It was a wonderful night for Beyoncé. She won three awards, all for "Crazy in Love," in the categories of Best Female Video, Best Choreography, and Best R&B Video.

Beyoncé then took to the road. She gave nine concerts in Europe in November. Two were at Wembley Stadium in London. They were filmed and later released as a DVD.

Then on February 1, 2004, Beyoncé fulfilled that dream she had had thirteen years earlier when she saw Whitney Houston sing "The Star-Spangled Banner" at the Super Bowl. Beyoncé sang the national anthem at Super Bowl XXXVIII in front of nearly seventy thousand people. And she sang it in front of her hometown friends and family, because the Super Bowl took place in Houston.

Two other singles were released from *Dangerously in Love*. Both hit the top ten on *Billboard*'s Hot 100 chart. In the spring, she ventured on another tour. This time, she was not the only star performer. Also touring with her throughout North America were female R&B artists Alicia Keys, Missy Elliott, and Tamia.

Later in 2004, Beyoncé, Kelly, and Michelle kept their promise. They reunited. The trio spent much of the year working on a new album.

In November 2004, the album *Destiny Fulfilled* was released. They were thrilled to be working together and decided the album would be all about sisterhood and love. Four singles were released from the album. Two, "Lose My Breath" and "Soldier," made the top ten on the Billboard charts. The album reached number two on the top albums chart. They toured together throughout much of 2005. The tour was called "Destiny Fulfilled . . . And Lovin' It."

When the tour was over, the singers had played sixty-seven concerts in sixteen countries, everywhere from the United States to Europe to Japan to Australia. Destiny's Child had come a long way since the days when they were giddy teenagers.

At a concert in Spain, Kelly announced on stage that Destiny's Child was breaking up for good. In a letter sent to MTV, the three members of Destiny's Child wrote, "After all these wonderful years working together, we realized that now is the time to pursue our personal goals and solo efforts in earnest."

In September 2005, an album of the group's greatest hits was released. The three members of Destiny's Child also showed their caring and love for others in a more meaningful way around the same time. A very strong and deadly storm, Hurricane Katrina, had killed hundreds of people and caused tremendous damage in Louisiana and Mississippi.

New Orleans was perhaps the hardest hit location, and thousands were flooded out of their homes. Many homeless were given shelter in the crowded stadium, the Superdome. Others were driven to Houston, about six hours away, for shelter. Kelly and Beyoncé's family set up a charity to help find temporary housing for those in Houston. They called it the Survivor Foundation, and Beyoncé alone donated $250,000.

About that time, Beyoncé decided to branch out beyond music and movies. She and her mother started up a new business—a fashion line. They called it House of Deréon. The name is a tribute to Beyoncé's grandmother, Agnez Deréon, a seamstress. The clothing includes sportswear, denim, and accessories, such as purses. The styles reflect Beyoncé's personal taste.

Soon afterward, she and Tina teamed up with a Houston footwear company called House of Brands. Together, they produced a line of shoes for House of Deréon. They also donated a portion of the money they made from House of Deréon products to help those made homeless from the damage of Hurricane Katrina.

Chapter 6

INTRODUCING SASHA FIERCE

Once more, it was the lure of the movie studio that attracted Beyoncé to her next project. A hit movie in 1963 titled *The Pink Panther* was a slapstick comedy set in the world of spies and detectives. The main character is a bumbling French police detective named Inspector Jacques Clouseau. In *The Pink Panther* and a few sequels, distinguished British actor Peter Sellers plays Clouseau. In time, Sellers became identified with Clouseau. Many who have not seen the movies in this series mistakenly think the Pink Panther is the nickname of a character. It is actually the name of a pink diamond.

It was decided in the mid-2000s to make a new Pink Panther movie. Peter Sellers had died years earlier, so they decided that veteran American comedian Steve Martin should play Clouseau. Martin is well regarded for his comedic acting and should be right at home in a slapstick comedy. Beyoncé was selected to play a superstar singer named Xania, the girlfriend of one of the other characters. Beyoncé really shines in the movie when her character sings.

The Pink Panther, starring Steve Martin, was released on February 10, 2006. Unfortunately, nearly all the reviews were bad. The common thread seemed to be that Steve Martin's performance was over the top. The critics remembered Peter Sellers's standout performances as Detective Clouseau and wrote that Martin was no Peter Sellers.

Audiences, however, saw the film differently. A new generation who knew nothing about the original Pink Panther movies with Peter Sellers thought Martin was great as Detective Clouseau. While they admitted that the new Pink Panther movie was not one of the world's greatest comedies, watching it was a fun experience. As a plus for Beyoncé, one of the songs she performed in the movie, "Check On It," made it to number one on the Billboard Hot 100 chart. It stayed at the top spot for five weeks.

Beyoncé spent most of 2006 working on another movie, *Dreamgirls*. It had once been a popular Broadway musical. *Dreamgirls* is based on the story of the highly successful 1960s female trio, the Supremes. The movie showcases the trio's rise to stardom and the drama that followed after they became successful. While the movie is based on the Supremes' story, it never claims to be a biography. For example, the girl group at the center of *Dreamgirls* is named the Dreams.

The lead singer of the Supremes was Diana Ross. She dominated the group so much that within a few years, they became known as Diana Ross and the Supremes. It has always been accepted by most in the music industry that the other members of the Supremes resented Ross for that. They felt she had become a diva. They believed that all three members should be treated equally—that no one should have top billing.

In *Dreamgirls*, the diva is named Deena Jones. That was the role played by Beyoncé. To prepare for the role, Beyoncé studied vintage film clips of the Supremes in concert. She also worked hard to lose weight and stay in shape so she could fit into tight gowns like those that the Supremes wore. After studying old clips of the Supremes, Beyoncé recognized that when performing, Destiny's Child had used some of the same steps and movements. She confessed to *Vanity Fair* magazine, "So basically, I've been training for ten years to be Deena." This being Beyoncé's first starring role in a movie, it was her chance to show the world what she could do.

Not being one to take things easy, Beyoncé used any spare time she had while making *Dreamgirls* to write songs for a new album. The album, titled *B'Day*, was introduced to the public at a party thrown by Jay-Z on September 4, 2006. It also happened to be Beyoncé's twenty-fifth birthday. Being a sharp businesswoman, Beyoncé used much of the time promoting *B'Day* on talk shows also promoting the House of Deréon fashions. The House of Deréon fashion line was expanded to include cocktail and evening dresses. Within a short time, House of Deréon fashions were being sold in department stores across North America.

Six singles were released from *B'Day*, but the biggest was "Irreplaceable." It is about a woman who discovers her boyfriend has been cheating on her. Instead of pitying herself, she shows a lot of resilience and becomes independent. The message of the song is that a strong woman doesn't need a man to be happy. She tells her ex-boyfriend that he is not irreplaceable.

"Irreplaceable" came out in November and went to number one on the Billboard Hot 100 chart. It stayed there for ten weeks. The official video also introduced to the public Beyoncé's new backup band. It consisted only of women and was called Suga Mama. Suga Mama played behind Beyoncé during live concerts on tour many times over the next several years.

Interestingly, "Irreplaceable" started out as a country song. However, with the production and arrangement efforts of Beyoncé and recording artist/record producer Ne-Yo, it sounds like pure rhythm and blues.

Meanwhile, *Dreamgirls* was released December 25, 2006. To the surprise of many, Beyoncé did not give the standout performance in *Dreamgirls*—Jennifer Hudson did. A former contestant on *American Idol*, Hudson played one of the other two members of the Dreams. This review by *Slate.com*'s movie critic, Dana Stevens, summed up most critics' reactions: "But the fact that even Beyoncé—a gifted and charismatic performer whose cheekbones alone are an argument for the existence of God—takes a back seat to Hudson throughout the movie is a measure of how star-making Hudson's supporting role is."

Hudson went on to win an Academy Award as Best Actress in a Supporting Role. Members of the Academy of Motion Picture Arts and Sciences, or members of the movie industry, give the Academy Awards annually. They are the oldest major awards in the entertainment industry, and to most people, they are the most respected.

The majority of film critics and moviegoers loved *Dreamgirls*. According to Internet Movie Database, the film cost $70 million to make and earned back more than $103 million. It is regarded as one of the most successful movies with an all African-American cast.

While she did not win an Oscar that year, Beyoncé did win a major award for her music. At the 2007 Grammy Award ceremonies, Beyoncé was rewarded for her hard work and creativity with a noteworthy honor: the prize for Best Contemporary R&B Album of the year for *B'Day*. She spent most of her time after the Grammys rehearsing for her next major tour.

It was a big one, lasting almost the entire year of 2007. The tour was titled "The Beyoncé Experience." It began in Japan on April 10 and ended in Las Vegas on December 30. Backing her up the whole time was her band of female musicians and ten dancers, five female and five male.

She made several side stops during the tour to conduct food drives for hungry people in cities, such as Washington, D. C.; Chicago; Los Angeles; and her hometown, Houston. In the midst of the tour, on June 25, she took another break to do a special concert with Jay-Z. It took place at the renowned Radio City

Music Hall in New York City, and it was given to commemorate the tenth anniversary of Jay-Z's hit album *Reasonable Doubt*.

Her September 2 show in Los Angeles was filmed to be sold as a DVD. The DVD was released to the public shortly afterward on November 20. A shortened version played on British television and in American movie theaters.

Beyoncé was nominated for a few more Grammy Awards at the 2008 ceremonies. Her nominations included "Irreplaceable" for Record of the Year. It did not win, but Beyoncé made headlines for a different reason at the Grammys. She and the legendary R&B singer Tina Turner did a duet of a song called "Proud Mary." Turner and her husband Ike Turner had a hit with it more than thirty years earlier.

Beyoncé was only in her twenties, but Turner was about seventy. Yet they both showed incredible energy in their performance, singing and dancing together. At one point during the duet, Beyoncé accidentally stepped on Turner's toe. But no one would ever have known since Turner kept on performing like the pro that she is. Caught up in the excitement of the moment, Beyoncé referred to Turner as "the queen."

That did not sit well with another music legend, Aretha Franklin. She has been known for decades as the Queen of Soul. According to *Sodahead.com*,

Franklin's publicity staff released the following statement on Franklin's behalf: "I am not sure of whose toes I may have stepped on or whose ego I may have bruised between the Grammy writers and Beyoncé. However, I dismissed it [calling Turner "the queen"] as a cheap shot for controversy."

It is interesting that Franklin used the metaphor of stepping on one's toes after Beyoncé literally had stepped on Turner's toe. Beyoncé's comment started a feud between her and the famed Queen of Soul. It has since been resolved.

Finally, after years of Internet rumors, Beyoncé and Jay-Z married each other on April 4, 2008. It was a small ceremony, with only family members and close friends as invited guests. The list included the two former members of Destiny's Child, Kelly Rowland and Michelle Williams.

While some observers think entertainers marry other entertainers because they have a lot in common, Beyoncé does not think that is always so. She said in the documentary Beyoncé: Life Is But a Dream, "I think maybe marrying a musician is a coincidence. We connected because we both perform and we both have similar lifestyles, but we connected on a spiritual level, and he just so happens to be a musician."

The day after the wedding, it was back to business for both. Jay-Z went back into a recording studio to make new music. Beyoncé returned to the scenes of two new movies she was making. One was titled *Cadillac Records*, the story of several blues and R&B greats in the 1950s and early 1960s. Beyoncé was chosen to play one of them, a multitalented singer named Etta James who rose to stardom in 1954.

James had fought drug addiction for much of her life. To prepare for the role, Beyoncé visited Phoenix House, a drug-addiction treatment center based in New York City. She talked with addicts in the process of recovering. She related, "It was very intense. Everyone was crying. These were women who had lost everything because of drugs."[1] She was so touched by the lives of those she met that she donated all the money she earned from the movie to Phoenix House.

The other was a thriller titled *Obsessed*. Not only did Beyoncé have a costarring role in *Obsessed*, she was also a producer. As producer, she supervised the making of the movie. She also furnished most of the money to have it made.

As she did in 2006, Beyoncé worked on writing songs for a new album during down time from making the movie. The album was released in November 2008. Actually, it was "albums," not "album," since it consisted of two compact discs. It was titled *I Am . . . Sasha Fierce*. The title raised two obvious questions: What did Beyoncé mean by that and who in the world is Sasha Fierce?

Sasha Fierce is the name Beyoncé gives her personality when she is performing onstage in front of thousands of fans. She explained, "My cousin Angie named her because I've kind of created a different person. If something's hard for me to do (in real life), when I get onstage, I do it without thinking. I don't remember some of the things I do onstage. Once at the MTV Awards, I had (a really expensive) bracelet on and chucked it into the audience. Angie had to go and retrieve it."[2]

Sasha Fierce is like a separate character from Beyoncé. If Beyoncé is the sweet, church-going girl who prays before every concert and is shy offstage, Sasha Fierce is just the opposite. She is the bold and brash Beyoncé, the woman wearing daring clothes and showing sass and independence in front of her fans. When she gets offstage, she returns to being Beyoncé.

I Am . . . Sasha Fierce consists of two CDs for a reason. The first disc is filled with songs performed by Beyoncé, the humble girl from Houston. The second compact disc is made up of songs reflecting the personality of the outgoing and tough Sasha Fierce. The first single released from the album was from the Sasha Fierce side. It is titled "Single Ladies (Put a Ring On it)."

It is a bouncy, catchy number. Like many of Beyoncé's songs, this one is also about empowerment for women. The song is a tale of a woman who gets tired of waiting for her boyfriend to make a permanent commitment to their relationship. She wants to get married, and he doesn't. If her boyfriend won't commit, she declares to herself that she is free to date others. She is looking forward to that because her boyfriend won't "put a ring on it." The Sasha Fierce side of Beyoncé does not take her boyfriend's lack of commitment sitting down. She goes out for a night on the town and shows her friends and the world that she does not need him.

"Single Ladies (Put a Ring On it)" went to number one on the Billboard Hot 100 and stayed there for four weeks. The official video for the song shows Beyoncé and two backup singers dancing to the song. The three long-legged women are wearing black leotards, and the dance moves are synchronized and intricate. The video was one of the most popular of the year.

Beyoncé's father, Mathew, told *Billboard* journalist Gail Mitchell he met the Sasha Fierce side of Beyoncé when she sang "Imagine" at the Houston talent show a long time ago when she was seven. He remembered how he and Tina could not believe that their Beyoncé was commanding the stage and charming an audience.

In the documentary *Beyoncé: Life Is But a Dream*, Beyoncé explained, "You look in the audience and you see this little girl. That was me when I was looking at Michael [Jackson] or Janet [Jackson] or Tina Turner. And there is no way I'm not going to give one hundred percent because I remember being that girl."

Her family and friends also might not have believed two other headline events in her life around that time. *Cadillac Records* first played at a few select theaters in late November 2008. By December 5, it was showing in thousands of theaters across the country. And in January 2009, she performed the classic romantic ballad, "At Last," for President Barack Obama and First Lady Michelle Obama at their inauguration ceremonies.

Many artists have recorded "At Last," but the best-known recording is by Etta James, Beyoncé's character in *Cadillac Records*. Critics' reviews of the movie in general were mostly positive, and Beyoncé's were mostly favorable. Comments made by Peter Howell of the *Toronto Star* were typical. He wrote: "Beyoncé doesn't show up as Etta James until well into the movie, but she floods the frame with the distilled pain of an R&B singer, known for her 1961 hit 'At Last.'" But for some reason, the movie was not popular with audiences. According to the Internet Movie Database, it cost about $12 million to make but earned back only a little more than $8 million.

Her other movie, *Obsessed*, was released April 24, 2009. Its reception was the opposite of *Cadillac Records*. It did make money. Internet Movie Database reports that it cost about $20 million to make and earned back more than $68 million. However, few reviewers liked it. Many thought the story seemed silly, predictable, and contrived. Even Beyoncé's performance was panned, although many said it was not her fault. They said the character she played was weak and clichéd. While she did show her ability as an action actress in a ten-minute-long fight scene, her character gave her little opportunity to display her acting talents.

Beyoncé was nominated for an award that was nothing to brag about. They are called the Golden Raspberry Awards, or Razzies. The Razzies are joke awards given to what one group sees as the worst acting performances of the year.

Beyoncé was nominated for a Razzie in the category of Worst Actress for her performance in *Obsessed*. While she did not win—the winner that year was Paris Hilton for *The Hottie and the Nottie*—Beyoncé learned that anyone in the entertainment business has to have thick skin. People are going to build them up but also tear them down.

That summer, Beyoncé took time to expand the House of Deréon. She and her mother added a line of back-to-school clothes called Sasha Fierce of Deréon. Yet in a couple of months, she would be the focus of another controversy—one she really had nothing to do with.

Chapter 7

SUPERSTAR AT
THE SUPER BOWL

Ⓘt was September 13, 2009, and the setting was the
MTV Music Awards. They were being held at the
famous and elegant Radio City Music Hall in
New York City. Nominated in the Best Female Video
category were both Beyoncé for "Single Ladies (Put a
Ring On It)" and pop-country singer Taylor Swift for
"You Belong With Me." Taylor Swift was favored to
win. And as expected, she did.

When her name was announced as the winner,
Swift walked to the stage and started to thank the
people who helped make her video a hit. She then told

the audience that she always dreamed of winning such an award. She added that because her music leans toward country, she never thought she would win an MTV award. Suddenly, in the middle of Swift's speech, Kanye West, a famous hip-hop star and collaborator with Jay-Z, left his seat in the audience and hurried to the stage.

He grabbed the microphone from her and said, "Taylor, I'm really happy for you, I'm going to let you finish, but Beyoncé had one of the best videos of all time. One of the best videos of all time."

A camera was quickly focused on Beyoncé while West was talking. She looked shocked and bewildered. Beyoncé mouthed something that looked like she said, "Oh, my God," or "Oh, Kanye." Beyoncé was clearly embarrassed. There she was, being put in an uncomfortable situation she had nothing to do with. As West left the stage, the audience booed him for what they saw as a rude action.

Swift was clearly uneasy. She never finished her speech and quietly walked off the stage. It did not matter that some people were not watching the show. The messy situation went viral on the Internet and was viewed millions of times.

Later on during the ceremony, twenty-eight-year-old Beyoncé won the award for Best Video of the Year, the most important award given at the MTV Music

Awards, for "Single Ladies (Put a Ring On It)." As she accepted the honor onstage, she announced, "I remember being seventeen years old, up for my first MTV award with Destiny's Child. And it was one of the most exciting moments of my life, so I would like for Taylor to come out and have her moment." Swift joined Beyoncé onstage and gave her acceptance speech. Beyoncé helped fix a bad situation. She showed she was a class act and cared about people's feelings. She also proved that she was not above sharing the stage with another star.

West apologized to Swift on Twitter and on *The Tonight Show With Jay Leno*. After some prompting, he called Swift to apologize personally. Swift praised Beyoncé for her grace and sensitivity. Swift then publicly said of Beyoncé, "It was just so wonderful and so incredibly classy of her." Beyoncé saved what would have been a snub to Swift, and she stopped an awkward situation from getting worse.

The year 2009 ended with bad and good news for Beyoncé. Her parents announced in November that they were getting a divorce. In a statement to the public, they said even though they would no longer be married, they would still be friends and business partners. But early in December, the Grammy Award nominations for the best music of the year were announced. Although she had been nominated for awards before, this time she accomplished something astounding. She was nominated for ten Grammys. Only Michael Jackson was nominated for more in one year when he received twelve nominations in 1984.

Beyoncé ended the year performing at a New Year's Eve party with Jay-Z and Usher. It took place on the Caribbean island of St. Bart's. The performers were told only that the concert was for some wealthy businessmen from abroad. Her performance at this concert later came back to haunt her in 2011.

Residents of several Arab-dominated countries in the Middle East and North Africa had been living in fear under strong-armed dictators for decades. Finally, many decided they had seen enough. Early in 2011, rebellions took place in some of those countries. Libya, which had been ruled with an iron fist by dictator, Muammar Gaddafi, for more than forty years, was one. Newspaper reporters searching for background information on the dictator discovered some fascinating facts.

One concerned the private New Year's Eve concert on the island of St. Bart's where Beyoncé performed more than a year earlier. The media learned that one of Gaddafi's family members was one of the concert's major promoters. Although it is likely that Beyoncé did not know that at the time, critics blasted her for performing for a dictator's family. It was embarrassing.

Soon afterward, one of Beyoncé's staff made a public announcement that any money she earned from the concert was donated to humanitarian groups helping the impoverished Caribbean island nation of Haiti rebuild after a disastrous earthquake. More than 300,000 people died as a result of the big quake or aftershocks.

As 2009 rolled into 2010, Beyoncé admitted to the public that she wanted to take a break from recording. She told *USA Today* that she needed time to "recharge my batteries." She did not take the time off to relax on a beach or at a mountain resort. Indeed, just a short time later, she was performing at a concert—but not just an ordinary one. Beyoncé was one of many celebrities who performed at a concert on January 22, 2010, called "Hope for Haiti Now: A Global Benefit for Earthquake Relief." Others included Alicia Keys, John Legend, Shakira, Stevie Wonder, Kid Rock, Taylor Swift, Madonna, and Jennifer Hudson. Beyoncé teamed up with Chris Martin of the band Coldplay to do a powerful rendition of Beyoncé's song "Halo." Martin played piano while Beyoncé sang. The concert was televised across the world, and its goal was to raise money from viewers to bring humanitarian aid to Haiti. More than $61 million dollars was raised.

Just a week later, on January 31, Beyoncé attended the Grammy Awards presentation in Los Angeles.

It was Beyoncé's night. She did not win in all ten categories in which she was nominated, but she did win six awards. In doing so, she set a record for most Grammy wins in one year by a woman.[1] Three were for "Single Ladies (Put a Ring On It)" in different categories: Best Female R&B Vocal Performance; Best R&B Song; and one of the biggest honors, Song of the Year.

After the wild success at the Grammy Awards, Beyoncé continued to expand her merchandise empire. She lent her name to a perfume released in February. Other female singers, including Britney Spears, Jennifer Lopez, and Gwen Stefani, had previously done the same. Beyoncé's fragrance was called Beyoncé Heat. The scent has been described as fruity, floral, and sweet.

At first, it was sold only at Macy's department stores. To promote the new product, Beyoncé made a personal appearance at the Macy's in New York City. As she signed autographs for fans, bottles of Beyoncé Heat flew off the shelves. According to *New York* magazine, 72,000 bottles were sold in one hour. And between February and early March, Macy's sold $3 million dollars worth of Beyoncé Heat. As talented as she was as a singer, she has proven to be just as savvy in the business world.

Other than doing a few concerts, Beyoncé kept to herself and took a break from work for most of 2010. She did not regret it. Beyoncé told *Cosmopolitan* magazine, "I've worked since the age of 15 and never taken any time out. My life has always been about next, next, next and moving on. I just decided to stop. It was the best decision I've ever made." She stated that she enjoyed spending much of the year hanging out with her husband, family, and friends.

Around this time, she made plans to act in another movie. It was to be a remake of a famous classic, *A Star Is Born*. This would be the fourth time it was made as a movie. It had been released as a film with different actors in 1937, 1954, and 1976. The original story is about an alcoholic actor near the end of his career helping a young girl find stardom. In the 1976 version, the character of the actor was changed to that of a fading rock musician. The past releases had women who were big stars in their time play the role of the up-and-coming starlet: Janet Gaynor in 1937, Judy Garland in 1954, and Barbra Streisand in 1976. Beyoncé would be in good company. The announced director was Clint Eastwood, one of the best in his craft.

In March, one of Beyoncé's staff members announced to the media that Beyoncé was no longer going to be represented by her father. She wanted to manage herself. In the announcement, Beyoncé was quoted as saying, "I grew up watching both he [Mathew] and my mother manage and own their own businesses. They were hard-working entrepreneurs and I will continue to follow in their footsteps. He is my father for life and I love my dad dearly. I am grateful for everything he has taught me."

The next day, Mathew released his announcement to the media. He said that he was fine with Beyoncé managing herself. He added that since she was almost thirty years old, it made sense that she wanted control of her business. Mathew continued, "Business is business and family is family. I love my daughter and am very proud of who she is and all that she has achieved. I look forward to her continued great success."

Some members of the media sympathized with Mathew. They thought it was a slap in the face to be let go by one's own daughter. Other observers were not surprised. They could see that Beyoncé was becoming more and more independent as she got older and her career reached new heights. Beyoncé said little about it afterward to the media or on her Web site.

She was happy to make a different kind of announcement soon afterward. It proved that despite controversies now and then, Beyoncé had become a true role model for young people. Beyoncé was proud to say that she was teaming up with the First Lady, Michelle Obama, on a special project. Most first ladies embark on a big volunteer project to help make the nation a better place to live. Michelle Obama's goal is to get children and teenagers in shape and to fight childhood obesity. What better person was there to help her stress her point than the energetic Beyoncé, who herself had struggled with weight issues?

In early May, she announced that she was teaming up with the First Lady to try to fight fat. The program was called "Let's Move! America's Move to Raise a Generation of Healthier Kids." To help promote the program, she changed the lyrics to her song, "Get Me Bodied" from the album *B'Day*. She retitled the song, "Move Your Body." The official video for the song featured Beyoncé, wearing jean shorts, a white shirt, green leggings, and high heels, dancing in a school cafeteria. Surrounding her is a crowd of dancing children of all ages with all kinds of bodies—from lean to overweight. It received more than 27 million hits on YouTube. Beyoncé also released a how-to video.

Beyoncé knows how hard it is for many to be comfortable with the way their bodies look. She admits she struggles with the same problem. Beyoncé confessed to James Patrick Herman of *InStyle* magazine, "I have days when I hate my hips and days when I feel good about myself. You just have to know what looks good on your body. I sure had to learn."

The next month her fourth solo studio album came out. It is simply titled *4*. Beyoncé says four is her favorite number. Her birthday is on the fourth. Her mother's birthday is on the fourth. Her wedding anniversary is on the fourth. And she says many of her friends' birthdays are on the fourth of various months. The album *4* hit number one on *Billboard*'s top albums chart the week it came out. She is one of only four musical artists to have her first four albums premiere at the number one spot on the respected *Billboard*'s albums chart. An astounding six singles from *4* were released.

At the MTV Music Awards, which took place on August 28, 2011, Beyoncé won another honor, for best choreography in a video for the song "Run the World (Girls)." To Beyoncé, the song has an important message. She explained, "We have to step up as women and take the lead and reach as high as humanly possible. That's what I'm going to do. That's my philosophy and that's what 'Girls' is all about."

Aside from her acceptance speech, she had another happy announcement to make to the public. Beyoncé told a national television audience that she and Jay-Z were expecting their first child.

She said when she was pregnant, "I don't know what God is trying to prepare me for, but I know that everything that's in my life is for a reason." She added, "Being pregnant is very much like falling in love. You are so open. You are so overjoyed."

Beyoncé gave birth to a baby girl on January 7, 2012, at Lenox Hill Hospital in New York City. The baby was named Blue Ivy Carter. Just two days later, Jay-Z released the song "Glory." It was dedicated to Blue Ivy and sounds of her crying were kept on the recording. Beyoncé took a few months off to rest and recover from childbirth. She made her first concert appearance as a new mother in late May at a casino resort in Atlantic City, New Jersey.

Her new role as a mother did not stop Beyoncé from tackling her other passions. In February, she launched a new fragrance called Heat Rush.

Everyone who had not been living in a cave for the past decade knew that because of her recordings, her movies, and her clothing and perfume lines, Beyoncé was wealthy beyond her dreams. *Forbes* magazine, dedicated to the world of finance and business, released its list of the wealthiest entertainers in 2012. Beyoncé was number sixteen on the list. *Forbes* wrote that she had earned $40 million in the past year. That total included her song sales, concert sales, House of Deréon sales, and product endorsements.

Forbes published a similar listing in their August issue. This one was of the world's richest celebrity couples. Beyoncé and Jay-Z were number one on the list. According to *Forbes*, the two had earned $78 million in the past year. By this time, it was hardly unusual to see Beyoncé's face gracing a magazine cover. There was something special, however, about her appearance on the cover of *People* magazine. *People* declared her the "world's most beautiful woman" in 2012.

Her third perfume, Pulse, was introduced in September. Eight months after the birth of Blue Ivy, Beyoncé was back to her busy schedule. She was so busy that she dropped out of making the movie *A Star Is Born*. Between their tight schedules, she and Clint Eastwood could not find the time to work together. She told MTV News, "I was looking forward to the production of *A Star Is Born* and the opportunity to work with Clint Eastwood. For months we tried to coordinate our schedules to bring this remake to life but it was just not possible. Hopefully in the future we will get a chance to work together."[2]

Beyoncé once more cemented her role as a superstar entertainer on January 21, 2013. She sang "The Star-Spangled Banner" at President Barack Obama's second inauguration. She impressed the audience—both in person and those watching on television—with her powerful rendition of the national anthem, a song many regard as tough to sing. Some critics said she should sing "The Star-Spangled Banner" at every presidential inauguration.

Shortly afterward, word started to leak that she had lip-synced, or mouthed the words, to a recording of the national anthem. The rumors spread, and in a short time, it became clear that it was true. It was humiliating for Beyoncé. Lip-syncing is often thought of as something done by amateurs, not seasoned professionals.

On January 31, 2013, she held a news conference where she admitted that the rumors were true—she had indeed lip-synced "The Star Spangled Banner" at President Obama's inauguration. However, before she spoke about the inauguration, Beyoncé showed that she has the chops to sing the national anthem live. She belted out a perfect rendition of "The Star Spangled Banner" to the audience of reporters at the press conference.

After she sang, she told reporters, "I am a perfectionist and one thing about me: I practice until my feet bleed. I did not have time to rehearse with the orchestra." She added, "Due to no proper sound check [test of sound equipment to make sure it is working properly], I did not feel comfortable taking a risk. It was about the president and the inauguration, and

I wanted to make him and my country proud, so I decided to sing along with my pre-recorded track."

Beyoncé was scheduled to sing and dance at the halftime show at the Super Bowl three days later in New Orleans. The Super Bowl halftime show is known for being a splashy extravaganza starring some of the world's best-known musicians. She assured the reporters she would sing live. Some reporters had heard rumors that her Super Bowl performance would include a reunion of Destiny's Child. Some had heard that Jay-Z would sing. She teased the reporters, saying simply, "I can't really give you any details. I'm sorry."

Even though Beyoncé admitted lip-syncing at the inauguration, some critics still were not satisfied. They continued to feel she deceived the American people by lip-syncing, even though she later admitted it publicly.

However, she convinced all doubters when she performed on Super Bowl Sunday. Sharing the stage with an army of dancers, a backup band with a stirring horn section, and a wild special-effects crew, Beyoncé sang many of her hits, including "Baby Boy," "Crazy in Love," and "The End of Time."

And sure enough, late in her set, Michelle Williams and Kelly Rowland rose up through a trapdoor in the stage floor. The reunited Destiny's Child sang

"Bootylicious" and "Independent Women." As they were thrilling the audience with "Single Ladies," Michelle and Kelly left the stage, allowing Beyoncé to finish her hit song as a solo act. Beyoncé finished the show with her power ballad "Halo."

Her halftime show received glowing reviews. John Caramanca of the *New York Times* wrote: "She filled the television screen, a human pneumatic drill of intensity, constantly bouncing and whirring. This is part of what set her apart from some past performers, whose songs were big enough, but whose attitude and presentation weren't."

Billboard magazine marveled, "A fierce and clearly possessed Beyoncé emerged from a cloud of smoke and lingering suspicion about her live-singing capabilities on Sunday, answering the doubters with an inspired display of hits and multimedia indulgence during her Super Bowl XLVII halftime show performance."

About two weeks later, the ninety-minute-long documentary about Beyoncé's life, *Beyoncé: Life Is But a Dream*, premiered on the pay-cable channel HBO. She directed and produced much of the project. The film begins with the camera panning across the newly mowed front lawn of her childhood home. The camera then focuses on the house. Beyoncé says over the scene, "I remember the moss on the trees.

I remember running through the sprinkler, summers, popsicles. I remember running as hard as I could. And my dad knew that I needed his approval. I think my father wouldn't give it to me because he kept pushing me, he kept pushing me, he kept pushing me. Every time my dad pushed me I got better and stronger."

Every part of her life, from her childhood to her work as an artist, businesswoman, and mother was depicted in the movie. There are scenes of her getting in shape and practicing with her dancers. Other scenes show her rehearsing on stage and being mobbed by fans at an airport. And there are shots of numerous concert performances. About an hour of the movie is devoted to her private and public life during her pregnancy.

Reviews were mixed. Some critics thought the movie showed personal moments in the life of a very private person. Others felt it was just a means of Beyoncé bringing attention to herself. Regardless, a huge number of viewers tuned in to see it. According to Gary Levin of *USA Today*, 1.8 million people watched it. It was HBO's most watched documentary in nearly ten years.

Beyoncé's overall respect as both a woman and an entertainer can be summed up by a chance meeting she once had in a public restroom with a woman she did not know. According to Elysa Gardner of *USA Today*, the woman recognized Beyoncé and said, "You're one of the only artists that my daughter and I both love, and I want to thank you for helping to bring us closer together." Beyoncé told Gardner, "That kind of compliment makes me feel so good."

There is no doubt she will be receiving similar compliments from fans as her superstar career continues.

Chronology

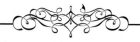

1981—Beyoncé Giselle Knowles is born September 4 in Houston, Texas.

1988—Wins first talent competition singing "Imagine."

1990—Begins attendance at magnet elementary school for children with musical talent; meets LaTavia Roberson and forms Girl's Tyme.

1991—Meets Kelindria (Kelly) Rowland who joins Girl's Tyme; meets LaToya Luckett who also joins Girl's Tyme.

1993—Group loses on television talent show *Star Search*.

1995—Group signed as Destiny, then dropped, by Elektra Records.

1996—Name of group officially changed to Destiny's Child; they sign contract with Columbia Records.

1997—Destiny's Child's first single, "No, No, No, Part 2," released; all leave public school to work full-time in the music industry and are taught by private tutors.

1998—Group releases first album, titled *Destiny's Child*.

1999—Second Destiny's Child album released, titled *The Writing's on the Wall*; first number one single, "Bills, Bills, Bills."

2000—All group members officially graduate high school; LaToya and LaTavia fired and replaced by Michelle Williams and Farrah Franklin; Franklin leaves shortly afterward; "Independent Women, Part 1" released, becomes Destiny's Child's most successful single.

2001—Destiny's Child awarded first Grammy for "Say My Name" as Best R&B Song of the Year; group performs at President George W. Bush's inauguration; Beyoncé stars in made-for-television movie *Carmen: A Hip Hopera;* Destiny's Child albums *Survivor* and *Eight Days of Christmas* released.

2002—Begins solo career; records first song with Jay-Z, "'03 Bonnie & Clyde;" acts in first movies made for theaters, *Austin Powers in Goldmember* and *The Fighting Temptations.*

2003—Released first solo album, *Dangerously in Love;* performs with Jay-Z at MTV Music Awards.

2004—Sings "Star-Spangled Banner" at Super Bowl; Destiny's Child reforms again for short time and releases album *Destiny Fulfilled.*

2005—Makes permanent break with Destiny's Child; establishes Survivor Foundation with family members and Kelly Rowland; founds House of Deréon.

2006—Appears in movies *The Pink Panther* and *Dreamgirls;* releases second solo album, *B'Day;* releases "Irreplaceable," which would become her biggest solo single.

2007—Receives Grammy Award for Best Contemporary R&B Album for *B'Day.*

2008—Marries Jay-Z on April 4; plays music legend Etta James in movie *Cadillac Records;* third solo album, *I Am … Sasha Fierce,* released.

2009—Performs at Obama inaugural ceremonies; wins Grammy Award again for Best Contemporary R&B Album for *I Am … Sasha Fierce;* lead role in movie *Obsessed;* incident at MTV Award ceremony involving Kanye West and Taylor Swift.

2010—"Single Ladies (Put a Ring On It)" wins Grammy Awards in three categories, including Song of the Year; plays controversial New Year's Eve concert.

2011—Wins six Grammy Awards out of ten nominations; begins managing her own career; fourth solo album, *4,* released.

2012—Daughter, Blue Ivy Carter, born on January 7.

2013—Lip-syncing controversy at presidential inauguration; sings at Super Bowl halftime show; Beyoncé documentary, *Life Is But a Dream,* released; plays Queen Tara in movie *Epic.*

DISCOGRAPHY & FILMOGRAPHY

Selected Discography

As Destiny's Child:
Destiny's Child (1998)
The Writing's on the Wall (1999)
Survivor (2001)
8 Days of Christmas (2001)
This Is the Remix (2002)
Destiny Fulfilled (2004)

As Beyoncé:
Dangerously in Love (2003)
B'Day (2006)
I Am . . . Sasha Fierce (2008)
4 (2011)

Selected Filmography

Carmen: A Hip-Hopera (2001)
Austin Powers in Goldmember (2002)
The Fighting Temptations (2003)
The Pink Panther (2006)
Dreamgirls (2006)
Obsessed (2009)
Epic (2013)

CHAPTER NOTES

Chapter 1: It Began With a Dream

1. Shirley Halperin, "Musicians React to Beyonce's Billboard Music Millennium Award," *Hollywood Reporter,* May 23, 2011, <http://www.hollywoodreporter.com/news/musicians-react-Beyoncé-s-billboard-191048> (December 7, 2012).

2. Steven M. Silverman, "Taylor Swift, Justin Bieber, Beyoncé Take Billboard Awards," *People.com,* May 22, 2011, <http://www.people.com/people/article/0,,20496607,00.html> (December 7, 2012), and Phil Gallo, "Ring the Alarm: Beyoncé Run the World," EBSCOhost, originally appeared in *Billboard,* June 4, 2011, <http://web.ebscohost.com/ehost/detail?vid=13&hid=125&sid=35e165b3-6747-4477-bbf5-e239baee31dd%40sessionmgr111&bdata=JkF1dGhUeXBlPWNvb2tpZSxpcCx1cmwsY3BpZCxjdXN0dWlkJmN1c3RpZD1rZWVuZXBsJnNpdGU9ZWhvc3QtbGl2ZQ%3d%3d#db=f5h&AN=61286771s> (August 15, 2011).

Chapter 2: "That Can't Be Our Beyoncé"

1. Toure, "A Woman Possessed," EBSCOhost, originally appeared in *Rolling Stone,* May 3, 2004, <http://web.ebscohost.com/ehost/detail?vid=4&hid=113&sid=35e165b3-6747-4477-bbf5-e239baee31dd%40sessionmgr111&bdata=JkF1dGhUeXBlPWNvb2tpZSxpcCx1cmwsY3BpZCxjdXN0dWlkJmN1c3RpZD1rZWVuZXBsJnNpdGU9ZWhvc3QtbGl2ZQ%3d%3d#db=f5h&AN=12339883> (August 15, 2012).

2. Ray Rogers, "The Billboard Q&A: Beyoncé," EBSCOhost, originally appeared in *Billboard,* June 4, 2011, <http://web. ebscohost.com/ehost/detail?vid=5&hid=11&sid=35e165b3-6747-4477-bbf5-e239baee31dd%40sessionmgr111&bdata=JkF 1dGhUeXBlPWNvb2tpZSxpcCx1cmwsY3BpZCxjdXN0d-WlkJmN1c3RpZD1rZWVuZXBsbndpdGctc3Qtb19lZ2Z Q%3d%3d#db=f5h&AN=61286769> (August 14, 2012).

Chapter 3: Good-bye Girl's Tyme

1. Kierna Mayo, "Beyoncé Unwrapped," EBSCOhost, originally appeared in *Essence,* August 2003, <http://web. ebscohost.com/ehost/detail?vid=7&hid=11&sid=35e165b3-6747-4477-bbf5-e239baee31dd%40sessionmgr111&bdata=JkF 1dGhUeXBlPWNvb2tpZSxpcCx1cmwsY3BpZCxjdXN0d-WlkJmN1c3RpZD1rZWVuZXBsbndpdGctc3Qtb19lZ2Z Q%3d%3d#db=f5h&AN=10302926> (August 14, 2012).

2. Mark Healy, "She Is Legend," EBSCOhost, originally appeared in *Marie Claire,* June 2009, <http://web.ebscohost. com/ehost/resultsadvanced?sid=35e165b3-6747-4477-bbf5-e239baee31dd%40sessionmgr111&vid=9&hid=122&bqu ery=TI+%28She+AND+%22is%22+AND+Legend%29&bdat a=JkF1dGhUeXBlPWNvb2tpZSxpcCx1cmwsY3BpZCxjdXN0d-WlkJmN1c3RpZD1rZWVuZXBsbndpdGctb1lhUiRiPWY1aCZ0eX-BlPTEmc2l0ZT1laG9zdC1saXZl> (August 14, 2102).

Chapter 4: Yes, Yes, Yes

1. Michael Hall, "It's a Family Affair," EBSCOhost, originally appeared in *Texas Monthly,* April 2004, <http://web.ebsco-host.com/ehost/detail?vid=14&hid=28&sid=35e165b3-6747-4477-bbf5-e239baee31dd%40sessionmgr111&bdata=JkF1dGh UeXBlPWNvb2tpZSxpcCx1cmwsY3BpZCxj.dXN0d-WlkJmN1 c3RpZD1rZWVuZXBsbndpdGctb19lZ2ZQ%3d%3d #db=f5h&AN=12686552> (August 14, 2012).

2. Danyel Smith, "Meeting Their DESTINY," EBSCOhost, originally appeared in *Teen People,* March 2001, <http://web. ebscohost.com/ehost/detail?vid=11&hid=28&sid=35e165b3-6747-4477-bbf5-e239baee31dd%40sessionmgr111&bdata=JkF 1dGhUeXBlPWNvb2tpZSxpcCx1cmwsY3BpZCxjdXN0d-WlkJmN1c3RpZD1rZWVuZXBsJnNpdGU9ZWhvc3QtbGl2Z Q%3d%3d#db=f5h&AN=7288294> (August 15, 2012).

Chapter 5: Beyoncé on the Big Screen

1. Mick LaSalle, "The Fighting Temptations," *San Francisco Chronicle,* September 19, 2003, <http://www.sfgate.com/ movies/article/FILM-CLIPS-Also-opening-today-2588118. php#page-1> (November 23, 2012).

2. Jeannine Amber, "Beyoncé's Destiny," EBSCOhost, originally appeared in *Essence,* October 2005, <http://web. ebscohost.com/ehost/detail?vid=16&hid=128&sid=35e165b3 -6747-4477-bbf5-e239baee31dd%40sessionmgr111&bdata=J kF1dGhUeXBlPWNvb2tpZSxpcCx1cmwsY3BpZCxjdXN0d WlkJmN1c3RpZD1rZWVuZXBsJnNpdGU9ZWhvc3QtbGl2Z Q%3d%3d#db=f5h&AN=26939659> (August 14, 2012).

Chapter 6: Introducing Sasha Fierce

1. Zach Jones, "Beyoncé Gives Back," EBSCOhost, originally appeared in *Scholastic Scope,* March 3, 2009, <http://web. ebscohost.com/ehost/detail?vid=20&hid=125&sid=35e165b3-6747-4477-bbf5-e239baee31dd%40sessionmgr111&bdata=JkF 1dGhUeXBlPWNvb2tpZSxpcCx1cmwsY3BpZCxjdXN0d-WlkJmN1c3RpZD1rZWVuZXBsJnNpdGU9ZWhvc3QtbGl2Z Q%3d%3d#db=f5h&AN=37274160> (August 14, 2012).

2. Lesley Rotchford, "Fun Fearless Female of the Year: Beyoncé," EBSCOhost, originally appeared in *Cosmopolitan,* February 2006, <http://web.ebscohost.com/ ehost/detail?vid=18&hid=19&sid=35e165b3-6747-4477-bbf 5-e239baee31dd%40sessionmgr111&bdata=JkF1dGhUeXBlP WNvb2tpZSxpcCx1cmwsY3BpZCxjdXN0dWlkJmN1c3RpZD 1rZWVuZXBBsJnNpdGU9ZWhvc3QtbGl2ZQ%3d%3d#db=f5 h&AN=19602989> (August 14, 2012).

Chapter 7: Superstar at the Super Bowl

1. Ann Donahue, "Beyoncé, Taylor Swift Score Big at 2010 Grammy Awards," *Billboard.com,* January 31, 2010, <http://www.billboard.com/news/Beyoncé-taylor-swift -score-big-at-2010-grammy-1004063905.story#/news/Beyoncé -taylor-swift-score-big-at-2010-grammy-1004063905.story> (December 6, 2012).

2. Jocelyn Vena, "Beyoncé Leaves Clint Eastwood's 'A Star Is Born' Remake," *MTV News,* October 10, 2012, <http:// www.mtv.com/news/articles/1695228/Beyoncé-clint-eastwood -star-is-born-movie.jhtml> (December 1, 2012).

GLOSSARY

a cappella—Singing without musical instruments in the background.

audition—Trying out for a recording contract or acting role.

contract—A legal agreement between people or groups, such as musical performers and record companies.

depression—A condition in which a person is severely sad, especially for a long period of time.

gig—A job for a musician.

inheritance—Money or objects designated by people before their deaths to give to family, friends, or others after their deaths.

lawsuit—A legal challenge filed by groups or individuals when they believe they have been wronged.

magnet school—A public elementary or secondary school that provides a unique or specialized curriculum in such a way as to attract a diversified student body.

manager—A person who helps performers make business decisions.

news conference—An interview of a famous person or people done by several members of the media.

production partner (in music)—One who works with others to design the arrangement of a song or album.

publicity—Information about a performer that is made public in order to make the performer better known.

remix—The alteration of an existing song to make the song sound different from previous versions.

single—A recording of just one song.

FURTHER READING

Books

Cartlidge, Cherese. *Beyoncé*. Detroit: Lucent Books, 2012.

Colson, Mary. *Beyoncé: A Life in Music*. Chicago: Raintree, 2011.

Easlea, Daryl. *Crazy in Love: The Beyoncé Knowles Biography*. London: Omnibus Press, 2011.

Vaughn, Andrew, *Beyoncé*. New York: Sterling Publishing, 2012.

Internet Addresses

The Official Beyoncé Site
<http://www.beyonce.com>

Biography.com: Beyoncé Knowles
<http://www.biography.com/people/beyonc%C3%A9-knowles-39230>

INDEX